SAVING CASPER

A Christian and an Atheist Talk about
Why We Need to Change the
Conversion Conversation

JIM HENDERSON
& MATT CASPER

TYNDALE™
MOMENTUM

An Imprint of
Tyndale House Publishers, Inc.

Visit Tyndale online at www.tyndale.com.

Visit Tyndale Momentum online at www.tyndalemomentum.com.

TYNDALE is a registered trademark of Tyndale House Publishers, Inc. *Tyndale Momentum* and the Tyndale Momentum logo are trademarks of Tyndale House Publishers, Inc. Tyndale Momentum is an imprint of Tyndale House Publishers, Inc.

Saving Casper: A Christian and an Atheist Talk about Why We Need to Change the Conversion Conversation

Designed by Mark Anthony Lane II

Published in association with the literary agency of Fedd and Company, Inc., PO Box 341973, Austin, TX, 78734.

Library of Congress Cataloging-in-Publication Data

Henderson, Jim, date.
    Saving Casper : a Christian and an atheist talk about why we need to change the conversion conversation / Jim Henderson and Matt Casper.
        pages cm
    Includes bibliographical references.
    ISBN 978-1-4143-6488-9 (sc)
1. Witness bearing (Christianity) 2. Evangelistic work. 3. Conversion—Christianity. I. Title.
    BV4520.H453 2013
    248'.5—dc23   2013012040

Printed in the United States of America

19   18   17   16   15   14   13
7   6   5   4   3   2   1

Jim: *To Brian McLaren and Father Joseph Fulton for teaching me that it's better to be kind than right.*

Matt: *To you, the person holding this book right now who is cherishing the well-being of others, no matter what they may believe.*

Contents

Foreword

I am not a big fan of categories, those real or imaginary boxes onto which we slap a definition or label so we have somewhere to put groups of people. Labeling is much easier than the messy discomfort that often arises out of relating to an actual human being.

I do acknowledge that boxes have a profound utilitarian purpose, whether it is for marketing, mission, misunderstanding, or manipulation.

Categories *can* be helpful in aiding our understanding and navigation through this cosmos in which we all dwell, but also powerfully divisive and destructive to relationships. Categories are both good and evil. It is important, for example, that children learn the difference between *me* and *them*, parent and nonparent, safe and not safe. But categories meant to establish helpful boundaries often turn into walls that frame prisons both for the "other" outside and we who are inside.

If I may use a word that I generally dislike, there is a *principle* regarding the difference between living inside fluid and dynamic organic categories and constructing inflexibly hard and defining boxes into which people and ideas are shackled—and from which any breath of life is exhaled. This truism is expressed in Jesus' potent statement that the Sabbath was made for human beings, not human beings for the Sabbath.

Even though the manipulation of consumer choice has become an intricate science in the realm of marketing and consumerism, marketing experts recognize that people are constantly caught in the flow of movement. The future is not the simple extrapolation of the past and present; there is a ghost in the machine—the human being who is fundamentally nondefinable and therefore part of the realm of mystery. However, less skilled and more brutal in its persistent construction of categories is the religious community.

It would be great if we lived isolated in a cave and could create all the boxes we wanted; no harm, no foul. But we don't. We live in community, and many of us battle against an entitled sense of moral and/or religious superiority and our tendency for cramming everything into tidy, mentally crafted boxes. The bigger complication arises when we are dealing with living human beings who don't fit so easily, and we feel compelled to cut off the extra bits that bother us or don't make sense.

One of the easiest religious expressions of "us" vs. "them" is the use of the two boxes "believer" and "unbeliever." Simple, at least in the way I grew up; Christians are in the believer box and everyone else isn't. But as we were educated in our Christian worldview, it became obvious there were people whom we thought were "believers" who began to defy the edges of our box, either because of their behavior or variances in their doctrinal theology. Now a decision had to be made regarding whether these people still qualified as believers or had slid back into the unbeliever box—or, easier still, had never been true believers in the first place. I was personally plagued with the nagging sense that the only real difference between myself and "them" was that I hadn't gotten caught yet.

The truth is, every human being is somewhere on the journey

between belief and unbelief. In fact, every belief implies unbelief. This is why questions themselves are so important, because they access our paradigms and rationalism and challenge us in our transformational journeys and relationships.

That's what Jim Henderson and Matt Casper do in this book: Ask questions. Challenge each other. Listen to each other. Care about each other. And relentlessly resist boxes of all kinds, choosing instead the path of learning together.

It doesn't end there. We have been taught all manner of new terminology—new theological and doctrinal words and meanings by which we begin to label the innumerable boxes upon boxes upon boxes. Some are prettier than others, some crude and rude, some slick and glossy. And with every reworked division, the believer box is reduced in size, the qualifications to be a member becoming more complicated and convoluted. Some boxes are easy . . . Mormon, Muslim, Buddhist, and Atheist, which are no-brainers, right? Some boxes, like that for the Jews, because of Jesus being their Messiah, have a secret door into the believer box—if not today . . . later. But even inside the believer box, there is plenty of uncertainty. This is especially true when we learn that the believer box is actually sealed and we may not really know what box we're in until the time of the grand future unveiling. So, we either work ourselves to the bone hoping to prove our worthiness, or we spend our lives perpetually in doubt.

I believe everyone is a believer, and everyone is an unbeliever. I believe that the Holy Spirit has been poured out, as the Bible says, "on *all* flesh." I believe we are called to tear down all the walls of these myriad boxes. I believe the living label we will place on the resulting, massively expanding and incomprehensively awe-filled box is "Jesus, the Incarnate Word of God," and that everything is by, for, through, and in him.

I know that Matt Casper is an unbeliever. (He is an atheist

after all!) I know Matt Casper is a believer—he told me himself. Let me share with you a few of the things Matt Casper believes. He believes in love: Not just any old blind romanticism, but other-centered, self-giving love. The love that exists inside him and is profoundly called out of him is most clearly seen in relationship to his children. Matt Casper also believes in life, this wonderfully intricate design of expanding elegance. Matt Casper believes in truth—that there are ways we are supposed to relate to one another that are simply indisputable. Matt Casper believes in evil—that many times the way we treat one another is wrong, absolutely wrong. Matt Casper believes that kindness is more real than abuse, honesty more than lies, dialogue more than division, authenticity more than hiding, integrity more than disintegration. Frankly, *Saving Casper* made me wonder if Matt Casper believes more than a lot of Christians.

What if believing is an activity and not a category? What if it involves beginning to see in such a way that our very being is freed to be the incredible creation that is true? After all, belief is not just a bunch of stuff the head thinks. Rather, belief is ascertained by the way in which someone lives life. It is expression, not ideology.

Saving Casper is the call to break down boxes and categories, revealing how to live out your beliefs through the bold and risky path of genuine, respectful relationship.

So, who is the believer now?

William Paul Young

Preface

JIM: Prior to writing *Jim & Casper Go to Church*, I had this idea that paying unchurched people to go to church and tell me what they think might yield some interesting insights into how nonbelievers view Christianity, and might give Christians an outsider's perspective on what we can do to improve our public image. This unusual hobby eventually evolved into a live event I called An Interview with Three Lost People, at which I interviewed non-Christians in front of a group of Christians.

This was how I first met Matt Casper. He was one of the lucky "lost" people I threw on stage in front of a room full of three hundred pastors. At the time, I knew Casper was "lost," but I hadn't yet heard that he was an out-and-out atheist. However, as fate would have it, he was. Casper's atheism wasn't a problem for me, but I knew it might be for many Christians.

One reason Casper's atheism wasn't a problem for me was that I already had plenty of experience with atheists. In fact, a few years earlier, I had been the winning bidder when an atheist college student named Hemant Mehta decided to auction his soul on eBay.[1] In exchange for my $504 "purchase," I asked Hemant to attend several church services, write reviews, and do radio interviews with me—which is where I first observed that many Christians had an unusual reaction to atheists. They seemed much more energized than they were around garden-variety "lost" people.

That's why I wanted to work with a real live atheist for the book I was planning. Simply put, atheists draw more attention from Christians than almost any other subcategory of non-Christian. Even more important, they provide a perspective on Christianity unlike any other group of nonbelievers—a perspective that can often be a blessing.

Samir Salmanovic, a Christian leader in interfaith dialogue, suggests that atheists are "God's whistle-blowers."[2] He explains the blessing that atheists can offer to religious people:

> Judaism, Christianity, and Islam need atheists, both those who are constructive and those who are less so. Religion deserves to be challenged. This deserving is of two types. First, religion *deserves the pain* of criticism and correction because of its failures to live up to its own ideals. Second, religion *deserves the blessing* of criticism and correction because it has often been a precious catalyst for justice, peace, and beauty in the world.
>
> God does not have an ego that can be wounded by our disbelief about God's existence. God, I suggest, would prefer a world where humans love and care for each other and this planet even at the expense of acknowledging God, rather than believing in and worshiping God at the expense of caring for one another and the world.[3]

If atheists are God's whistle-blowers, I knew I needed one to help me with my project—to help us Christians live up to our own ideals. That's why I asked Casper to join me.

A couple of years after we first met on stage during An Interview with Three Lost People, Casper and I decided to keep our conversation going. I told him I wanted him to attend some of America's largest churches and give me his unfiltered feedback. I told him I was a former pastor and a follower of Jesus, but that I would not be trying to "save" him along the way. If he got saved, that was on him. We detailed this story in our first book together, *Jim & Casper Go to Church*.

Saving Casper is, to some degree, a continuation of the conversation we started in *Jim & Casper Go to Church*; but, more important, it is the ongoing story of our friendship and mutual quest for understanding. In it you will find many questions remain unanswered and many more bubble to the surface. But in those questions are some solutions we hope will begin to change the conversation about conversion, faith, church, and God, and how they relate to all of us.

Introduction

JIM: After reading *Jim & Casper Go to Church*, many people said there was one question Casper asked that kept echoing in their minds. Following almost every church visit—after seeing, in many cases, the spectacle, the lights, the music (and in one case, an actual fog machine)—Casper would turn to me and say, "Jim, is this *really* what Jesus told you guys to do?" A simple question that I think many Christians today are still trying to answer.

Casper's words are certainly blunt, but I'm sure they resonate with you. Maybe you've wondered, as I have, why we Christians talk about, but rarely measure, how we're doing with our mission to reach "lost" people. Maybe it's because we're not doing as well, or as much, as we say we're doing. Whatever the reason, from my perspective, this is exactly why we *need* people like Casper—to tell us the truth as they see it. Of course, his feedback is subjective—insights from one person who is outside the church—but if we don't look outside the church, how else can we determine how our mission to *reach* people outside the church is going?

As I see it, if feedback from atheists such as Casper can help us reach the world for Christ, then why not listen to what they have to say? Also, based on my experience with other atheists, I believe they are uniquely qualified to critique us. Here's why:

- Many atheists put the Bible in the same category as *Snow White and the Seven Dwarfs*—as a fairy tale—a viewpoint that is especially important to hear for those who have grown up in a belief system that unequivocally accepts the Bible as God's Word.
- Atheists have zero brand loyalty to Christianity or any other faith-based system, so they're quicker to call out artificiality and manipulation.
- Many atheists believe that religion in general is actually *dangerous* for mankind. Given the fact that Jesus never instructed His followers to go into the religion business, it helps to have someone notice when we're getting a little too comfortable with the religion label.
- Because Christians often claim the moral high ground from the stance of our biblically based beliefs, atheists can help keep us grounded by asking us questions like, "Is this really what Jesus told you to do?"

Those are my perceptions. However, what I believe about atheists may not be what they believe about themselves. Luckily, I have a friend named Casper, who happens to be an atheist, and I get to ask him directly.

Here's the number one thing Christians say to me behind Casper's back: "Jim, I appreciate your desire to 'connect' with him, but give me a straight answer. Is Casper saved yet?"

Here's why I think Christians ask this question: They've been taught to value above all else something that didn't especially concern Jesus—namely, the finish line (a.k.a. the prayer of salvation). But if we use as our standard what I've come to think of as a "finish-line fixation," we'd have to agree that Jesus was an evangelistic failure.

In John 4, we see Jesus engage in a conversation with a Samaritan woman and illustrate the ways in which religion can be good. One could assume (after all, this is Jesus!) that the conversation would naturally culminate with Jesus challenging her to repent, or in modern-day evangelical parlance, "accept Him as her personal Savior."

But that's not what happened. Look closely at the exchange and you'll see the genius of Jesus, the master *discipler*, at work. The Samaritan woman tosses Jesus an evangelistic softball when she says, "I know that Messiah" (called Christ) "is coming. When he comes, he will explain everything to us." Then Jesus declared, "I, the one speaking to you—I am he" (John 4:25-26). The Samaritan woman sets up the perfect opportunity for Jesus to convert her, but He simply reveals that He is the Messiah and leaves the ball in her court.

Jesus is unquestionably bold in asserting His Messiah-ship, but He fails to challenge the woman to cross the finish line. Because you and I know the end of the story, and because this is Jesus we're talking about, we give Him a pass. However if this were a case study for Evangelism 101, Jesus would get an A for boldness and . . .or follow-through.

Here is a person who could easily get run over by a stray water buffalo on her way back to the village, and yet Jesus lets her go without closing the sale. The Samaritan woman was practically begging for Him to call her down to the altar, and instead He lets her walk. I believe Jesus simply obeyed the impulses the Holy Spirit put in His heart. He let the Holy Spirit take the lead.

Jesus called people to follow Him, to be His apprentices. Conversion is *part of the process*, but it's not the first step. Often it's not clear exactly when the conversion threshold is reached or how it comes about. It's mysterious. Ask your friends and you'll hear a hundred different stories about how they "came to Christ."

We do know how human beings are apt to change, and it

doesn't match up with the way Christians have been trained to engage with nonbelievers.

You might say, "But thousands of people are coming to faith every week in churches all over America. We see them on TV!" And you would be correct, but millions more are staying home. We don't see *them* on TV.

I have had some pastors suggest the following: "Well, that's their fault, Jim. There are plenty of churches for them to go to." Again, they're right on the nose, yet the people vote with their feet by propping them up on Sunday and playing video games.

In Matthew 28:19, Jesus doesn't mention anything about people going to church; rather, He directs His followers to go out and make disciples. Jesus did not need to use manipulation, fear, or force to win hearts. He simply demonstrated love. And when Christians embody the Christ they want others to see, it's always a good thing.

Jesus never led anyone to the altar and never guided anyone through the "Sinner's Prayer." But that wasn't His goal. He didn't set out to make converts; He sought disciples. In fact, He seemed far more interested in the *starting line* than the finish line. Jesus didn't tell us to *save* anyone: He told us to *make disciples*. And the difference between *converts* and *disciples* is simple. Getting someone to agree with us is a lot easier, and yet more fleeting, than convincing someone to "take up their cross and follow."

With that in mind, I would ask some direct questions:

- When was the last time you led someone to Christ, personally praying with them to accept Christ as their personal Savior?
- How many times in your Christian life have you actually led someone to Christ?
- How many people have you yourself discipled, starting

with the prayer of salvation and studying with them as
they matured?

- When was the last time you invited a coworker, friend, or
fellow student to church with the expectation that they
would come back?
- How many people have you not invited to church because
you weren't sure how to explain it to them?
- Have you really memorized as much of the Bible as you
should to be equipped for "convincing" your friends that
they should accept Jesus?

Harsh? Maybe. But if we are to understand what is really happening in our efforts to convert people, and how to make conversion "stick," we have to be brutally honest with ourselves about expectations and reality. How many of us want to have to answer the most difficult questions that everyone who cares about evangelism will face:

- Has anyone you loved and tried to witness to died without
accepting Christ?
- Do you feel responsible for their likely eternal destiny?
- Has this motivated you to double down, study harder, and
witness more, or to pull away, feel bad, keep the sense of
failure to yourself, and essentially drop out of evangelizing
altogether?

I believe that millions of Christians suffer from what I call Evangelism Frustration Disorder (EFD). Do these symptoms describe your evangelism experience?

- Chronic guilt over your unwillingness to "witness" to your
friends and family.
- Spiritually debilitating depression over your "lack of
boldness."

- Obsessive channel surfing and book buying to find the coolest new evangelism program.
- Anxiety when the pastor mentions evangelism or the great commission.
- Giving money to "on fire" Christians who *will* witness to assuage your feelings of guilt about *not* witnessing.

If researcher George Barna is right, the vast majority of evangelical Christians might actually be suffering from EFD. A Barna survey of non-Christians showed that

- 4 percent had been invited to attend church with a friend, and had;
- 23 percent had been invited to attend, but declined;
- 73 percent had *never* been invited.

Barna concludes: "Perhaps the most obvious observation is that most unchurched people are not being pursued by anyone."[4]

This leaves us to ask, "Why?" Why aren't ordinary Christians—people who say they care deeply about reaching non-Christians with the Good News—inviting people to church?

Here's my best guess . . .

Something has changed culturally. As technology has bridged the distance between us, it has also created a more insular society in which people don't connect personally. More and more, connection happens in a digital vacuum. But it's not all bad news for the church. Sociologist Robert Putnam thinks he sees a silver lining in what many Christians imagine is a cloud of doom for organized religion in America.

In a report by Dan Harris of ABC News, Putnam says it's possible that the current spike in young people opting out of organized religion could also prove to be an opportunity for some: "America historically has been a very inventive and even entrepreneurial place in terms of religion. . . . Jesus said, 'Be fishers of men,' and there's this pool with a lot of fish in it and no fishermen right now."

"In the end," Putnam concludes, "this 'stunning' trend of young people becoming less religious could lead to America's next great burst of religious innovation."[5] It's through innovation that we are most likely to win converts, but innovation is never—and I mean *never*—achieved without a few failures along the way.

It is this turning point that brings me to the purpose for this book. It isn't to answer the question of the state of Casper's salvation. It isn't to offer a tutorial on how to successfully snatch the soul of an atheist from the grasp of Satan. Our purpose is to swing open the doors of communication and demonstrate how honest and respectful conversation can open more hearts than all the preaching, Bible quoting, and fear mongering ever will.

For this reason, we have chosen to structure the book as a discussion in which I, Jim, will be the moderator, raising questions for Casper to answer and offering insights that we hope will allow each side to peer into the world of the other for better understanding and relationship building.

CASPER: I don't remember if I identified myself as an atheist when I first met Jim for his "Interviews with the Lost" thing. All I knew was that he was looking for "lost" people and I thought it was probably best to just call myself "lost" rather than "atheist" because the latter label seems to scare the pants off a lot of people.

When Jim called me later to see if I wanted to audition for his next project, traveling to churches and writing what eventually became *Jim & Casper Go to Church*, he asked if I was an atheist. I remember having to think about it. Am I? I ran down the list of qualifications to be an atheist, as I saw them: Do I believe in a supernatural God? Currently, no.

Turns out that, for me, the list of what it takes to be an atheist is pretty short. So I remember saying to Jim, "Yeah, I believe I am an atheist. . . . I hope that's not a problem." Jim said, "No problem. I basically need you to be an atheist for this project. So are you ready for an adventure?"

I said yes, obviously, and the good part then (and now) was that I really wasn't sure what to expect from this adventure—which made it ideal, as there was no way I could be disappointed. No expectations = no way to be let down. To me, it sounded . . . well . . . fun. Traveling a bit throughout America with a guy who seemed pretty cool—nonjudgmental, intellectually curious, into music. I figured I could count on Jim not being up in my face with the, "Have you thought about where you'll spend eternity?" thing the whole time. I figured I was safe from the hard sell.

It's not that Jim never shared his faith with me or that I was opposed to hearing about it. Actually, I was (and still am) interested, probably because he was also interested in me and what I believed in and cared about. We talked about feelings more than faith, music as much as God, and we found some common ground.

It made me wish that more people would just take it easy and introduce their faith a little more slowly. I have realized in talking with Christians over the past few years that no one is going to keep the attention of a nonbeliever by starting a conversation with Bible verses and language a nonbeliever can't relate to. It's common sense, really: If you want to engage with someone, you have to speak their language first. That's what I do . . . for the most part, anyway.

But what really made this project most appealing to me

was that, like most human beings, I was and am very curious about the Big Questions: Why are we here? What's the meaning of life? What happens after we die? And if exploring these questions would take me to about a dozen buildings where the people inside said they had the answers—or, at least, that's what I thought I would experience—well, that sounded pretty cool. As it turned out, I wasn't given The Answers—not even wrong ones. What I was met with was the old hard sell and the Hollywood-style hard sell in some cases.

I didn't get it then, and I don't think I get it now. I just remember thinking at the time, *Wow . . . bummer. Most of these churches are basically businesses.* Sure, many of the people we met along the way were people of deep and unwavering faith, but from my vantage point, they had that faith whether they were in a church service or not.

And when we ended up writing about our Sunday visits where I got these first impressions, plenty of people took us to task, saying, "It's not fair to judge a church based on a single Sunday visit."

I say, "What?" because I always thought the Sunday morning church service was the preferred point of entry for outsiders—the place where Christians proclaim, "Hey, outsiders! Come on in! See what our God and our faith are all about!" So like Jim, I thought a Sunday visit would be the ideal time for a church and its people to share their faith, but that's really not what I found.

Instead, most churches were about loud music, bright lights, and demands for money . . . at least that's my main memory. I also remember sermons that seemed less about what it means to be a Christian than about how hard it is to *stay* a Christian—like "Don't Stop Believing!" which really only made me think about a "small town girl living in a lonely world." And again, the main things I remember from some of the megachurches were the appeals for money.

I don't remember Jesus asking for money. As a matter of fact, there's something in the Bible about not being able to serve two masters, right? But at some of these giant churches—with their waterfalls and TV shows and gift shops and private-plane-flying preachers—it seemed like they'd picked master #2.

Jim referred to me as his "whistle-blower." I would probably just call it unfiltered feedback from someone outside the fishbowl, as it were. Otherwise, it seems to me that books written by evangelicals *for* evangelicals to help evangelicals connect with non-evangelicals are like an auto repair manual written by someone who has never seen or sat in a car trying to explain how to drive or fix a car to someone else who has never seen or sat in a car. When the basis of your argument comes from a point of reference that is alien to the other person, you are stalled out of the gate. Seeing as there is nothing most churches would like more than a chance to save folks like me from whatever it is you think I need saving from, I'd think that some honest feedback would be useful.

JIM: So that is what Casper offers us: *honest feedback*. You'll see as we progress through this conversation that Casper will be straightforward and honest about his observations. As anyone who has met him knows, it isn't because he's trying to be critical or to beat up on Christians. I believe it's truly because he wants to give us all a glimpse of what he sees, in hopes that it will help us clarify our message and intentions.

WHAT'S WRONG WITH JIM?

JIM: Before we can explore how Christians can better relate to their atheist friends, neighbors, and family members, it is important to address some of the common misconceptions Christians have about what atheists think. As Casper and I traveled and spoke with Christian groups, certain questions came up time and again. These are also the questions I mentioned in the introduction, so let's give Casper an opportunity to answer them here because they not only reveal the preconceived notions that many Christians have about "godless atheists," but they also prevent many believers from even daring to start a conversation with a nonbeliever, and they stand in the way of our ability to communicate effectively with nonbelievers when they gather enough courage to trust us with their questions.

Casper, we've heard that atheists see the Bible as a fairy tale, and that people like you think the Bible is complete fiction. True or false?

CASPER: I know there are some atheists and other nonbeliever groups who see the Bible—and the Koran and the Talmud and the Book of Mormon—as a collection of fairy tales, but there's no way that applies to all of us. Personally, I know there's a lot of history to be found in the Bible and there's a lot of help to be found in it as well. I don't disagree with much of it at all.

I will confess, though, that I struggle with people who believe every word to be 100 percent true from beginning to end since there are so many contradictions. I always wonder how these folks reconcile the discrepancies. There are blogs and entire websites devoted to explaining these complications, but the "Sunday school" answer usually seems to be that mankind can't divine the will of God (but the blogger or website author will certainly give it a shot!)

From some atheists' perspectives, well, those contradictions are used as proof that the whole Bible is malarkey. I think it's a moot point, but I also think it might help some Christians to keep in mind that using the Bible as some form of "proof" is a nonstarter for most nonbelievers. Christians need to remember that nonbelievers also "non-believe" the Bible, and perhaps even "non-believe" the Bible more than they "non-believe" in God.

Speaking for myself, I think the Bible has a lot of important, moving, and wonderful stories, but there are also a lot of rules that may have applied back then but don't really apply now. (I mean, come on: How many Christians are really following the command not to wear clothes of mixed fiber?) But the best part of the Bible for me has always been the words of Jesus.

Jesus' words, as recorded in the Bible, make almost uniform sense to me, except for the supernatural components. (But I feel the same way about the teachings of Buddha: It all makes sense except the reincarnation parts.) And Christianity is really all about Jesus, right? I mean, it's *His* name on the box.

So though I may struggle with many aspects of the Bible, most of what Jesus said is inspiring and enlightening for me. And one thing all our church visits taught me is that the Bible can be used in these discussions the way some people use statistics: selectively. And now, like so many of the pastors we saw during our church visits, I, too, find verses from the Bible to support what I'm saying and gloss over those that don't.

JIM: My relationship with Casper is partially a learning experiment. I frankly consider it a privilege to hang out with someone (whom I believe) Jesus loves, and have him tell me as we go along the path together what he is and isn't experiencing relative to my perceptions. I want to closely compare and contrast my social construction of reality with his, and this begins with his perspective on the tenets of the faith I want him to embrace.

If I don't *hear* Casper, if he's simply a target or an object of my evangelistic desire, what do I do when he fails to fulfill my expectations? What do Christians do with nonbelievers as a whole? Where do we start if we can't defend our faith with the very handbook that we were given to instruct us? Well, Casper has given us a pretty big hint on that one: Jesus.

Some Christians believe that atheists unfairly target Christians over other people of faith. What do you say about that, Casper?

CASPER: First I would ask, Is this an accurate perception? Maybe it is, but I prefer to look at things on a case-by-case basis. Some might say Christianity is the most hypocritical faith—for example, many Christians in America claim to worship a God of love, but at the same time they're okay with gross prejudices, violent discriminations, and mass murder by the military—and therefore maybe Christianity is the most worthy target.

Some might say that most atheists are former Christians, with damage, and that is what makes them categorically hate Christianity. Others might say Christianity is "safe" to target because going after Islam in a similar fashion could quickly get ugly and violent.

For me, I just understand Christianity more than any other religion and therefore have more specific questions about it. I was raised in America and attended church as a child. I even went to a Catholic college, though not for the Catholicism. I have never been Catholic. I didn't even know what Ash Wednesday was about, so imagine my surprise freshman year when I suddenly saw everybody walking around with ashes on their foreheads. I'd point it out—"Hey, you have some dirt on your head"—and they'd say, "Ha-ha, very funny," and I'd say, "No, really, you do!" I felt like I was in the twilight zone.

Anyway, I am definitely experienced with the Christian "brand." And maybe this makes me—atheist or not—qualified enough to speak about the issues I have observed in American Christianity, having been raised around it.

But just because I know far more about Christianity than I do about Islam, for example, doesn't mean I have "brand loyalty" to it or to any faith more than another. When you're an atheist, you don't have a horse in this race. When someone says they believe in an all-powerful God—and I don't believe in gods of any kind—why would I say one god I don't believe in is better than another god I also don't believe in? And in this case, it looks to me as if Christianity and Islam are worshiping the same God anyway.

I think it can actually be a benefit (even an honor) to have so many nonbelievers more interested in Christianity than perhaps any other faith, because, when handled well, their interest gives you more opportunities to share what you believe and why.

JIM: Sharing your faith is intimidating on a good day, but going up against people who are well-known for their faith (or lack of it) is a whole other level of scary. Have you ever had the opportunity to "Save a Celebrity"? Someone famous, like Bob Dylan or Lady Gaga. Well, I have! I am going to tell you this story as an illustration of a choice we have. The direction we choose to go has a direct correlation to perpetuating the perceptions of Christianity that Casper just covered.

In 2009, I was invited to do an interview with Ira Glass, host and creator of *This American Life*. Ira is one of America's best storytellers and a certifiable rock star to about two million people who avidly follow him on the radio.

He was famous, he had an audience, he was an atheist, and he was asking *me* about evangelism! Here was my big chance to "Save a Celebrity"! How did I do? You can listen to the interview in the *This American Life* archives, but let me spare you the digging and the wait.

Realizing that millions of people would be listening and that God might be giving me this unique opportunity to "preach the gospel" to an audience of exceedingly difficult-to-reach cultural elites who definitely skew non-evangelical (read: *seriously* unsaved), I basically bombed. Here's how the conversation went.

> **Ira:** Jim, isn't it true that your version of evangelism actually leads to *nothing*?
>
> **Jim:** Ira, as I see it, I have two scenarios. Scenario 1 is I "witness" to you and valiantly attempt to save you right here on the radio. But if history is any indicator, and barring a true miracle of divine intervention, you

will most likely reject my offer. I then go back to my supporters and claim victory, even though you said no, because our evangelism paradigm provides me an "out."

As long as I *try* to save you, I still get "points" for being courageous enough to boldly preach the gospel. Another evangelistic loophole I can use is to claim that Jesus said people (especially famous people like you) would reject me. So even though you remain lost and on your way to my hell, I actually win! And, oh, one other thing: *You and I will never speak again*. But hey, this is spiritual warfare and losing a possible relationship with you is simply collateral damage.

In scenario 2, I say something like, "Ira, is there anything that I believe to be true about Jesus that you want to know more about?" I'm transparent and direct. I keep things real without placing undue pressure on our relationship. Instead of my pushing something on you, this approach requires that you *pull* something from me. You say yes or no and I answer. If you're interested in following Jesus right now, I say, "Cool, let's talk or pray." And if you say you're not interested in following Jesus right now, I say, "Cool, let's grab a coffee and talk about your show." You and I continue to hang out and learn from each other and see what happens.

I told Ira, "I choose scenario 2 every time."

I said this not because I was afraid to give him *my personal testimony* or tell him about Jesus. I'd already done that with hundreds of people. Nor was it because I was trying to be progressive, relevant, or postmodern. And it's certainly not because I don't believe in conversion.

I chose scenario 2 for a simple and very strategic reason:

People typically come to faith (or buy a car, choose a school, or invest their money) as the result of an influential relationship with someone they trust and are conversant with.

So you see, we can either continue to give nonbelievers ammunition for their aversion to the faith, or we can back away from our conversion checklists and leave doors open for them to walk through as they grow more curious.

Casper, do you think there is anything useful in religion? Some atheists say that religion is always dangerous.

CASPER: Always dangerous? Of course not! The best thing I ever heard about this—and I don't remember where I heard it—was that religion is a good thing for good people and a bad thing for bad people. It's totally subjective. For example, I love it that Jim has faith. It drives him to help others. I hate it that a guy like Fred Phelps, the leader of Westboro Church in Kansas, who pickets at the funerals of AIDS victims and soldiers killed in combat, has faith. His so-called faith drives him to behave monstrously.

You can point to the wonderful things Christians do to serve others and make the world a better place. You can also point to the bloody slaughter of the Crusades. I don't think there's anything but a subjective answer to the question. Religion is a good thing when it inspires people to help others. But it has also proven to be a very bad thing in many other ways.

Casper, what about your team's version of Fred Phelps? (Yes, I'm talking about Richard Dawkins.) Would you agree that atheists are the ideological enemies of Christians?

CASPER: Good grief! *No!* Different does not mean we're at odds. I mean, come on! I am very different from my children, but we're not enemies. Women are different from men, etc. And as far as Christian ideology goes . . . well, it seems to change from person to person, so I have to consider people on a case-by-case basis. I think anyone who calls himself a Christian would be well served to do the same with atheists: *case by case.*

I can understand why Christians might consider Richard Dawkins their ideological enemy as he does nothing but attack them; but don't lump me in with him. And I will do the same. I consider Fred Phelps my ideological enemy—because he seems to stand only for discrimination and seems to think it's appropriate to share his twisted views when people are at their most heartbroken—but by no means do I consider all Christians to be my enemies.

And I know some folks think I've been hard on prosperity preachers; but the truth is, I do not consider them my ideological enemies. I see them more as Jesus' ideological enemies, since it seems they are using Jesus' name to make themselves wealthy.

JIM: One of the most influential books I've read is called *To Change the World.* In it, professor James Davison Hunter analyzes what it actually takes to "change the world." He suggests that Christianity suffers from idealism:

> Idealism misconstrues agency, implying the capacity to bring about influence where the capacity may not exist or where it may only be weak. Idealism underplays the importance of history and historical forces and its interaction with culture as it is lived and experienced. Further idealism ignores the way culture is generated, coordinated, and organized. Thus it underrates how difficult it is to penetrate culture and influence its direction.[6]

Perhaps more than any other Christian practice, modern day evangelism beliefs and practices emerge out of the mix of idealism and denial concerning the agency of sin, culture, and complex human experience. The inflexibility of so much idealism is what produced the Crusaders and people like Fred Phelps, who put such horrible black marks on the history and perception of Christianity.

This same attitude is what makes people such as Richard Dawkins just as ineffectual. Are you okay with alienating everyone you are trying to influence just to make your point? Are you content to feel you've made a good argument at the expense of potential relationships? It's one thing to have a set of ideals you strive toward; it is another thing to be so stringently idealistic that there is no room for individual experience.

Do you think Christians are failures if they don't fully embody Christ? In other words, do atheists expect all Christians to act just like Jesus?

CASPER: Isn't that what being a Christian is all about? You don't have to be an atheist to expect Christians to act like Jesus. You only need to be able to read the Bible.

JIM: That pretty much says everything we need to know. Of all the directives, missions, callings, and charges, the one thing—the *only* thing—we are really expected to do is show others why we claim Jesus, why we want others to know Him. If we aren't doing that, and if Casper is a good barometer of the view from the other side of the fence, then we can't possibly expect atheists to have an interest in being on the bandwagon.

However, the reason this feels so daunting is because of the *false belief* many of us have been taught: "When conversion is done right, it is dramatic and instantaneous."

We have this image in our heads because modern-day evangelicalism has put it there, meaning the preponderance of salvation stories that are preached, printed, or produced for Christian TV are fast, furious, and fantastic.

But in my experience, that's not how things typically go down. The truth typically has a bumpier road, one filled with unexpected stops and detours. Have you ever heard an evangelist tell a story like this?

"When I was six years old, I went to the altar. When I was ten, I walked away. When I was sixteen, I got saved at youth camp and then when I went to college, I dropped out and started taking drugs. I lived with a girl for five years and she got saved, and for five more years I said no. Then I lost my job, so I asked my girlfriend and her church friends to pray for me. I got a job, so I felt guilty and started coming back to church, and I recently gave my heart to the Lord, but I'm not one hundred percent sure about the whole tithing thing and Jesus being the only way and all that stuff."

You haven't heard a story like this because it's "too normal," and if evangelists are anything, it's "not normal." We Christians like our evangelists to be different and *on fire.*

You're lost, then you're found, then you're filled with God's love and spread the Good News until you die and join God in heaven. No wavering or wandering allowed.

The only problem is that's not how people usually experience faith or come to faith. The fact is, for most of us, faith is fluid. Researchers Nick Spencer and Peter Nielson tell us:

Wandering is part of the journey itself. We do people's stories and indeed the whole business of "finding faith" a disservice if we envisage it as a simple, predictable, linear path, from which we deviate at a cost. Awkward as it may be, people's journeys are personal, unpredictable, unique,

and marked by meanderings. Sometimes, walking away
from the path is part of the journey.[7]

People are open to new religious experiences and are experi-
menting with them more than ever. When someone says they're
Wiccan, Christian, or atheist, it might be more accurate if they
added the word *currently*, as my friend Casper does. (If you read
Jim & Casper Go to Church, you may recall that this is one of
the first things he ever said to me—that he was "currently an
atheist"—because he believes, as I do, that beliefs and faith are
fluid and subject to change.)

People wander in and out of different faith experiences,
including atheism, agnosticism, and Christianity. My hope has
been to shine a friendly but powerful light on the fallacy that
conversion is a straight-line kind of experience because statistics
and stories prove that it's actually a squiggly line.

In 1992, an exhaustive study of over five hundred Britons
who had come to faith in the previous twelve months found
that sixty-nine percent described their conversion as gradual.[8]

The gradual process is the way in which the majority of
people discover God and the average time taken is about
four years: models of evangelism which can help people
along the pathway are needed.[9]

It bears repeating what researcher John Finney found in his
research: *"Models of evangelism which can help people along the
pathway are needed."*

I have been encouraging and developing models of evangelism
that help people along the pathway for the past fifteen years.
I've often done this in collaboration with other people who take
chances with the ideas the Holy Spirit puts in their hearts; but as
with all inventors, many of my ideas end up on the floor.

However, like the path that led from the Palm Pilot to the iPhone, if you aren't willing to fail, you really aren't willing to even try. Failure is the only way you can, in some wonderful cases, *succeed*.

As you can see, Casper is his own kind of atheist. Or as he has told me many times, he's someone who "happens to be an atheist." He's unpredictable and unabashed, and in his own words, he's "okay with being wrong. . . . You usually learn something then, right?" Perhaps he's a lot like you.

Followers of Jesus who sincerely care about connecting with what I call "the people Jesus misses most" need a new map, something that helps us navigate relationships with people like Casper. It is my desire for all people to know Jesus. I want Casper to know Jesus. But if in the process of trying to make Jesus plain to him I become artificial or mean, then I've stopped being like Jesus.

I used to think that if I lost a friend in the process of evangelizing, it was okay with Jesus. But if I do that, pretty soon I'll end up with no non-Christian friends and no one to evangelize. I no longer believe this is the outcome Jesus had in mind when He told us to apprentice people in the ways of His Kingdom.

That's why this is not another evangelism how-to book. Instead, we're exploring the unseen but incredibly valuable world of how to have a transparent friendship with someone who holds a very different view of life. This is also why I'm writing this book *with* Casper rather than *about* Casper.

With Casper, I enjoy a fresh set of eyes to help me see our world from a completely different perspective. In this book, we share not only what we learned from our church visits, we also share what we learned from our personal visits with each other as friends, business partners, and co-explorers.

And Casper—somewhat in response to what so many people

have asked me but mostly as part of our growing connection and relationship—shares with me just what he thinks it might take to "save" someone like him.

For some readers, the success of my "experiment" can only be measured by the status of Casper's eternal soul, and they won't be satisfied with anything less than a cut-and-dried, tied-with-a-fancy-ribbon solution. Life is rarely that neat and tidy, and the journey of faith is never straight and narrow.

Albert Einstein once said: "Everything that can be counted does not necessarily count; everything that counts cannot necessarily be counted."[10] From a mathematical perspective, that is perplexing. From a spiritual perspective it's as simple as understanding what really matters in God's eyes.

In a fascinating book called *Zero: The Biography of a Dangerous Idea*, Charles Seife explains that at one time the number zero was actually considered dangerous. "The Greeks so despised zero that they refused to admit it into their writings, even though they saw how useful it was."[11] Why? "Zero clashed with one of the central tenets of Western philosophy. . . . The whole Greek universe rested upon this pillar: there is no void."[12]

The only cultures that allowed zero in their numeric systems were Arabs and East Indians. The Greeks and those influenced by Greek thinking rejected this "invisible" or intangible number because allowing it into their thinking would imply not knowing. This would also allow for a universe that was not closed—and by extension, no longer controllable by the religious authorities.

As Seife points out, the Greeks believed that "within zero there is the power to shatter the framework of logic."[13] Consequently, they blocked its usage in the West for more than two thousand years until eventually the advancement of knowledge and the need for better technology demanded its acceptance.

In similar fashion, during the time of Jesus, the Pharisees

feared His "invisible" counting system. Jesus took small things—ordinary people and unspectacular events, such as having dinner with someone or spending a few minutes with a woman who interrupted Him on His way to heal a young child—and turned them into big experiences in people's lives.

God "counts" differently from the way we do. He sees the invisible realities and how they influence the visible relationships we live in. He isn't afraid of including invisible numbers—unknown factors—in His counting system. God's values are different from ours. God's economy operates on capital that doesn't fit in our system. God keeps records using an entirely different rubric.

My hope is that through this conversation, you will see a new way of counting what God counts. Most of all, I want you to know that your life with God counts, and that, just like Jesus, you can follow the Holy Spirit on this adventure of connecting with the people Jesus misses most so they can discover His winsome and powerful love.

YOU SEEM REALLY NICE. . . .
TOO BAD YOU'RE GOING TO HELL

JIM: Before we wrote *Jim & Casper Go to Church*, the typical "Christian and atheist" connection (if there was one) was probably a debate. Since neither Casper nor I enjoy debating, we decided to do something different. We chose to visit churches, write reviews, be curious about each other's viewpoints, and share our unvarnished impressions with the world.

We did establish some ground rules—namely, his opinion regarding churches is correct for him; mine is correct for me. We agreed to focus on the common ground in our experiences more than the differences in our beliefs (hence our beginning most church reviews with the easy stuff—the lights, the music, etc.—before getting into the meaning of the message). We decided to use this experience to *learn* from each other. And while this idea seemed straightforward to us, it proved to be provocative enough to attract quite a bit of attention, including some Christian radio shows. Call-in radio shows can feel surreal. As the interviewee, the experience can be both exhilarating and depressing.

Casper and I typically called in from different cities, breaking away from our day jobs to get on the phone with a radio host we'd never spoken with before. "Drive Time Dave" would cut away from his show during a commercial break.

"Hi, Jim, is it true that you bought an atheist's soul on eBay? Are you 'that guy'?"

"That's me, Dave, but Casper the atheist is *not* the eBay atheist. They're two different guys."

"Great, that's just great, Jim . . . great to have you and 'Casper the eBay Atheist' on today."

And with that, Casper and I would be put on hold as Drive Time Dave prepared his listeners for what often felt to Casper and me like becoming the punch line to one of those "A Christian and an atheist go into a bar" jokes, at best, and a couple of freaks whom callers were encouraged to attack, at worst.

What follows is Casper's take on the experience.

CASPER: As an atheist trying to be kind and open-minded on Christian radios shows that could occasionally turn combative, the experience was often bewildering.

There was a whole "celebrity" component that was fun. It always felt good to get the call from radio producers, telling us they'd love to have us on to talk about our book, our experiences, and so on . . . and then they'd open the phone lines so that people could call in . . . and tell me I would be burning in hell for all eternity.

Usually, the host would say, "We're now gonna take a few questions from our listeners," but more often than not it turned out to be a few condemnations instead.

"Hi, Dave. This is Gary from Spokane, and I just want to say to Casper that he's going to hell." *Click.*

"Hi, Dave. This is Lewis from Eugene—longtime listener,

first-time caller—and I just want to say to Casper that he's going to hell." *Click.*

"Hi, Dave. My name is Marianne and I live in Spokane as well. I really enjoyed the show today. Jim, I think it's important work that you're doing. It's not everyone who has the courage to mix and mingle with atheists and other nonbelievers, and in one sense there's much we can all learn from your efforts."

"Thanks, Marianne. Anything you'd like to say to Casper?"

"Absolutely! Thanks for having the courage to share your ideas with us. I think you have wisdom, are a kind person, and will burn in hell."

That was the gist, no matter how nice—or not nice—people were, they seemed resigned to the notion that Satan would torture me for all eternity, which is something I simply have an impossible time getting my head around.

I began to think they sounded like they were happy I was going to hell. Where were they coming from? Why were they able to discuss my eternal torture in such casual tones? And why, even when they would profess to be concerned with salvation, did they still seem less focused on my being saved for endless eternity than on my being *wrong* in the here and now?

I was under the impression that Jesus came to show people a better way to live—you know, love your neighbor, feed and clothe the poor, do unto others, etc. But when you throw hell into the mix, it tends to take center stage. I mean, we're talking flames and burning for eternity. We go from "I think this, you think that, let's discuss our differences" to a scenario where my head is on a pike in the blackest pit of Hades.

JIM: Jesus did come to show people a better way to live, Casper, and depending on which set of church teachings you follow, Jesus came for myriad other reasons as well.

Now some readers are probably thinking that, as an atheist, Casper is predisposed to characterizing the Christian callers as a bunch of hell-focused crazies. Well, let's just say that while Casper may be taking some editorial license with his recall (as we all do), the issue of hell was raised often enough to make me cringe. I was embarrassed by the predictability of Christians bringing up— and often *leading* with—the hell question.

The anonymity afforded by our invisibility on the radio probably served to embolden these believers, who most likely would never ask that question if they had to look Casper in the eye. I asked Casper about this "scaring evangelism."

CASPER: I'm sure the church has gotten plenty of converts by scaring them. There are two ways to get what you want from someone, right? Carrot or stick, reward or punishment. Maybe when it comes to saving people, the short-run gains are easier with the threat of punishment or damnation than with the hope of reward and salvation.

But it always felt like damnation was an arrow in the quiver of any Christian I would speak to. I could see it there, waiting, and I knew that if we reached an impasse in our conversation—*whoosh!*—out would come the hell arrow. *"In closing, let me just say (1) hell, (2) going to, (3) you are."* It never bothered me much, though, because I had the words of Jesus to protect me from this argument and the people who would make it: *"Judge not, that you be not judged."* Worked every time!

JIM: Casper nails the problem with the *scaring* approach to evangelism—it isn't working. Despite all the PR hell has received, it has nevertheless failed to scare the majority of nonbelievers into church or faith in God. In fact, I think an argument could be made that most nonbelievers have heard so much about hell that they've become desensitized to the idea. To be sure, a few folks may still be motivated by the threat of eternal damnation—and I'm certain it worked even better hundreds of years ago—but it's simply not that effective today.

I think even more important, it has been a statistical flop at motivating rank-and-file Christians to do more evangelizing. I mean, think about it: If you truly thought the world was going to end tomorrow, wouldn't you feel obligated to get out there and warn all your friends, not to mention your family members?

Believing in the current evangelical version of hell is kind of like that. We say that everyone who hasn't accepted Christ as Savior will go to hell, yet we sit in front of TVs, play video games, go out to dinner, play with our kids, and track our investments online. No wonder nonbelievers don't think we really mean what we say about hell. If we did, we would be living a very different kind of life.

Even Jesus appears to have had a somewhat laid-back approach to hell when you consider He spent the first thirty years of His life living a very private existence and—one could say—"doing nothing." I believe some people might be better served by doing (or saying) nothing. When Casper and I spoke at an event in Kansas City, a woman stood up and said to me, about Casper, "Why are you making this church into a platform for *his* evil?"

CASPER: She acted like I was evil incarnate—and I'd never even met her before. All she knew was that I didn't believe what she wanted me to believe . . . and she didn't give a damn about saving me, apparently. She just wanted me to go away—and whether that was back home to San Diego or down into hell . . . well, I don't believe it really mattered to her at that moment.

I could see that Jim was about to shut her down to spare

me from her attack, but I asked her to keep talking. Heck, wouldn't anyone want to learn why they were considered evil, assuming they didn't already know? I mean, it was only after our book came out that I realized there were a lot of people who were certain I was going to hell. There were just so many voices in agreement on the subject. But the more I listened, the less it all made sense.

I think the first time I heard someone say I was going to hell, my instinct was to be reactive, like, *"Well, same to you, pal!"* And that reaction is a natural feeling when someone you don't know insults you. I think I can speak for most every nonbeliever out there when I tell you we hear a lot more than concern for our immortal soul when you "warn" us about hell. We typically hear something along the lines of, "You're a horrible person who deserves eternal punishment." How would you feel if someone said they thought you should suffer for eternity just because you don't agree with them?

However, as I've gotten older and wiser, or perhaps because of my unusual circumstances—being an atheist who speaks at churches—I know there's something behind all that venting, and it's usually something more hopeful than hell.

Maybe it's just that something in me has changed. Maybe I prefer to see the glass half-full, to find something hopeful . . . or maybe I just don't feel the need to tell people off quite so much. Whatever it is, I've found that life becomes a lot more interesting when I don't take the bait. So I started applying this principle to folks who told me I was on my way to hell.

I can only guess what they anticipate my response will be when they say I'm going to hell. Perhaps I might say, "Fine!" or "No such thing!" or "No, *you* are going to hell." Instead, I started asking, "Why?" and this opened the door to discussing their beliefs, which I always find interesting.

I feel as if I'm still a student in many ways. It's like those late-night conversations you have when you're in your late teens or early twenties, where you question the nature of existence, stare at your hands, stretch out your thinking, and let your mind be blown. I think that's what it is for me. I am always looking for someone to stretch my thinking.

When I've taken time to listen, even recently, to people who were cheerfully consigning me to hell, I've discovered that most people don't come by their beliefs lightly. Something has happened to them—an event occurred somewhere along the line that was truly transformative. It is deeply personal for them. I respect that. I want to hear more about that.

JIM: This is exactly the kind of openness and curiosity I'm hoping more *believers* will engage in. I'm simply trying to follow Jesus, and here is what I've learned from Him about how to think about this dilemma. *Beliefs* about hell and other mysteries are important, yes; but they're not nearly as important as *practices*.

Beliefs are the principles that *inform* our practices. Beliefs are the *information* that leads to *formation*. Jesus was far more focused on *formation* than He ever was on *information*. That's what He meant when He said, "Therefore everyone who hears these words of mine and puts them into *practice* is like a wise man who built his house on the rock" (Matthew 7:24, emphasis added).

The hell-centric evangelism approaches that enable Christians to dehumanize, objectify, and dismiss people who disagree springs from a "beliefs first" gospel. That's why one guy on the phone could say he liked Casper and then when he felt rejected, flippantly add, "Have fun in hell." Because Casper rejects his beliefs, he rejects Casper, who is no longer a person to him; he's only a target.

CASPER: You know, people who are trying to save others by using the promise of heaven or the threat of hell might want to keep in mind that promises and threats only work if both parties agree on the legitimacy or value of the threats or promises. For example, if I train my kids to look both ways before crossing the street, but they never once see a car whiz by, they will probably wonder why I'm so concerned about dangers that, from their eyes, don't exist at all.

As an atheist, it's kind of hard to explain this to Christians. The point is, most people don't worry too much about things they don't believe exist. To use an utterly absurd example, imagine if you told your friends, "You need to serve lunch to the homeless every Tuesday, because if you don't, a unicorn death squad will ravage your home." Would these folks feel in any way compelled to serve those lunches? Probably not. Because most folks don't believe in unicorns, let alone unicorn death squads.

The threat of hell hanging over the head of a person who doesn't believe in it doesn't really accomplish anything at all . . . other than maybe pushing that person away.

JIM: *Apologetics* is a technical term that involves "defending the faith," a term that is strangely misleading and insightful. Most Christian "apologists" are focused more on forcefully defending their faith than on listening to nonbelievers or apologizing to them for how some Christians have badly represented their faith. As with most humans, we Christians don't want to admit we're wrong or say we're sorry. It could make us look weak, and make God look like He doesn't know what He's doing.

Remarkably, however, whenever I've genuinely apologized to non-Christians for the non-Christlike behavior of Christians, it has had just the opposite effect. It doesn't result in my giving up ground. In fact, people become more open, more curious. I think there should be a whole evangelism program built around training Christians how to apologize without being defensive. Maybe we could call it "evangelize with your ears."

CASPER: I remember talking on a radio show to a guy whom Jim later referred to as a Christian apologist. The main thing I recall the "apologist" saying to me was, "How can you look at the ocean and say there's not a God?" That's a pretty standard question or pitch from believers to nonbelievers. If we're to follow the standard script, my response should be about the big bang and how the oceans were an "act of science," and how anyone who doesn't respect science has his head in the sand, and so on. But for some reason, I decided to tell the caller what happens to me when I look at the ocean: I'm awestruck. Amazed. Filled with a sense of wonder. It's no different for me than for anyone else. I decided that sharing my natural reaction would be far more interesting than arguing with the caller about how we felt when looking at the ocean. That made as much sense to me as arguing about how it feels to look at Van Gogh's *Starry Night*. Am I going to claim that someone else's emotional response is less valid than mine? Is that what Jesus would do?

I can just imagine the scene:

Me: Jesus, it's a truly beautiful morning. The sun streaking through the trees at daybreak fills my heart with joy.

Jesus: Wrong, Casper. You may *say* it fills your heart with joy, but your joy isn't as real as *my* joy. Also, you're going to hell.

Back to the caller and his question about the ocean. I told him it's not like I look at the ocean and say, "Ah, what a beautiful ocean. There is definitely not a God." No, I look at the ocean and let my mind run. I think about the depth and breadth of life in it and across the planet. I think about how unique the planet is, how it's just the right size and just the right distance from just the right-sized star, how water could cover it, how life could grow. How there are literally billions of stars and—so far, and as far as we know—this is the only place where this extraordinary thing called *life* occurs. And here we are, billions of years later, talking on a radio! Driving cars! Using wi-fi! Doesn't that blow your mind? Isn't that as wondrous a story as this all being created by an unseen, all-knowing entity?

When I said that, the line went silent for a bit, and then he said, "Yeah, that's interesting. Too bad you're going to hell."

I'm not sure what to do with people like this. It's as if they'll give me the one pitch they have, and then because I don't just say, "Wow! You're *right*! The ocean *proves* the existence of God!" now I'm going to hell. Really? That's all they've got?

JIM: The sad news is that some of the Christians we've run into are like people who have only one tool in their toolbox—a hammer. For them, every problem is a nail. So no matter what you say, they *see* a nail and attack it with force. And if you reject their approach, they simply declare that you lack the ability to see that your problem is a *nail*.

Going back to the story of Jesus with the Samaritan woman at the well, we see the master evangelist had other tools in His toolbox. Jesus didn't follow an evangelistic program or have a set of evangelism principles. Instead, He followed the Holy Spirit.

To use a poker player's expression, it was the Holy Spirit who told Jesus when to hold 'em and when to fold 'em. This is why even though Jesus telegraphed His hand to the woman, He didn't call her to show her hand. The Holy Spirit had bigger fish to fry in the woman's village. The Holy Spirit was after the whole town and He knew that this woman would be His evangelist.

We observe the Samaritan woman's sense of being in control

of her own destiny and newfound feeling of personal worth when she invites the whole village to "come, see a man who told me everything I ever did" (John 4:29)—as if this were good news! Jesus and the Holy Spirit tag-teamed this woman and brought her to repentance using what the apostle Paul refers to as "God's kindness" (Romans 2:4). Together, they collapsed her defenses and drew her to bring many others to Jesus' heart. Jesus, of course, was unafraid of their differences.

CASPER: Here's what I can't figure out: Why do different beliefs seem to frighten so many Christians? A lack of interest leads to a lack of understanding, which often leads to fear. And fear leads to most every other problem in the world. Where's the harm in being curious, in asking questions?

And if Christians are truly tasked with saving others, how can they expect to even start down that path without first being curious about the inner lives, feelings, and values of the people they're trying to save? It would be like going to the doctor for a checkup and instead of examining you, the doctor just tells you where it hurts.

"Doctor, I have a pain in my arm."

"You mean your ear."

"No, it's more along my arm here."

"I'm the doctor. And I'm telling you it's your ear that hurts. And if you disagree with me again, you can go to hell."

JIM: I've been astounded to discover how people generally lack curiosity about other people, other beliefs, other perceptions, and other ways of making sense of reality. Christians claim to be following the one true God, who has transformed us and given us an eternal and abundant life. We, of all people, should be the most curious, the least threatened by differences, and the kindest people on the face of this earth.

It seems, however, that we've become more concerned with being *right* than with being kind. I often like to illustrate this gap to my Christian brothers and sisters by rephrasing 1 Corinthians 13:13, a very popular passage from the Bible that anyone who has attended a wedding is likely to be familiar with: "Now these three remain: faith, hope, and love. But the greatest of these is *truth*."

CASPER: Isn't the greatest supposed to be *love*, Jim?

JIM: It's supposed to be, but somewhere along the way we've lost our focus, even when we claim to be searching for lost souls out of love. As we continue this conversation, reclaiming that message will be our aim.

CALLED TO QUESTION

JIM: I have found two reliable ways to learn if a person qualifies for a long-term friendship: spending money together or traveling together.

Since our first book came out, Casper and I have done both. We've traveled together to several churches and college campuses, as well as to a Young Life camp in Oregon, and we've spent money together by going into business and starting our own website, called ChurchRater (more on that later).

On our first road trip, Casper and I entered churches anonymously. We sat in the back, typed away on our laptops, and for the most part were ignored. However, this time out, people put us on a stage and put a microphone in our hands. I was admittedly more than a little anxious about these events. As we saw in chapter 2, Christians can be so unabashed in the expression of their beliefs that it can border on cruelty and abuse. I considered how I could guard my friend Casper from those attacks.

At the same time, I wondered if I would need to be a buffer or offer protection for our Christian audiences if Casper decided to respond in kind and go on the attack, like Richard Dawkins. I knew Casper wasn't "that kind of atheist," but in front of a large crowd of people who might be verbally assaulting him, well, maybe he would reach for something other than consideration and humor for ammunition.

Though I didn't know what or whom Casper was going to lean on, I knew I was about to learn how to trust Jesus on a deeper level than ever.

I have some friends in Boulder, Colorado, who invited us to speak to their campus group. We showed up to a standing-room-only crowd—which, in typical college kid fashion, meant that bodies were strewn all over the floor. We had to step over people to find a place from which to address the group.

Casper got to Colorado a couple of days before I did to see his mom, who lived in the Denver area. She had recently converted to Catholicism and led the choir at a large Catholic church. She had also recently been diagnosed with cancer. Sadly, and soon, Casper's mom lost her fight with the disease.

I remember Casper's mom being so weak she had to lie on a couch, but she made sure she was there to hear her son speak. Of course, her lounging made her fit right in with all the college kids. I remember thinking that it was nice of them to leave the couch for her. I could see the light in her eyes as Casper spoke. She was so proud of him.

CASPER: I found out my mom had AML—acute myelogenous leukemia—in 2007. I remember when she called me and told me she had some bad news. She sounded like she had been given a death sentence, but I didn't immediately comprehend it. At the time I thought, *Leukemia? That's one of the ones that can be beat, right?* But as I dug more into what it all meant, I felt my heart grow heavier and heavier.

I know that as I share this, some Christians may be think-ing, *That's when you let God into your heart, so that He may raise you up*; but that just didn't make sense to me at that point in my life even though, like more than a few agnostics and atheists I've spoken with along the way, I often wish it did. The truth is, unlike me, my mom had God in her heart, her friends had God in their hearts . . . and *all* of us were heart-broken by this.

My mom had begun chemotherapy right around the time we were in Boulder. She still had all of her hair, but her energy was vastly depleted. And it was hard for me to see her like that. My most vivid memories of my mom always involved her being active. We were going on a hike or for a bike ride. We were going on a so-called rafting excursion—which, as I recall from the perspective of the curmudgeonly eleven-year-old boy I was at the time, was a day spent sitting in a sludgy swamp being eaten alive by deer flies. So seeing my mom constantly exhausted was not something I was accustomed to. But she soldiered on nonetheless and was with us at that event in Boulder.

JIM: I was very curious about Casper's mother's spiritual search. Since he is an atheist, I not only wondered how she felt about his lack of faith, but also how she had raised him and especially about her own later-in-life conversion to Catholicism. Casper told me that when he was growing up, his mom would take him to various churches where she sang as a paid soloist. He went to Congregational, Presbyterian, Unitarian, and finally Catholic churches, with a brief stint on his own at an Episcopal church where he was in the boys' choir. I began to wonder, in all of this exploration, if his mother had ever contemplated atheism as an option.

CASPER: I never once heard my mom say anything but that she believed. However, one day in early 2007, after *Jim & Casper Go to Church* came out and she'd read it, she said to me, "I have been fighting atheism for most of my life." I took that to mean—perhaps because of the relatively combative side of Christianity I had recently experienced—that she had been taking on atheists in the streets by carrying placards or handing out evangelistic tracts. I was shocked.

When I asked her about this, she clarified, "No, *within myself* I have been fighting atheism." This surprised me because my mom was always involved with some form of religious faith over the years. She checked out many faiths, as well as a few churches. There was what I called my mom's Summer of New Age, which followed her divorce from my dad. I remember visiting her at the Omega Institute for Holistic Studies—which still exists and is still "the nation's most trusted source for wellness and personal growth"—and learning about crystals, chakras, and all that.

Also, there were Buddhist statues in our house when I was growing up. I remember partying with my friends in the kitchen as a teenager, trying to figure out the meaning of a poster on the wall that had Japanese characters and a phrase in English: "Sitting quietly, doing nothing."

There was even a foray into Scientology along the way. I remember seeing the book *Dianetics* around the house and thinking it was about dinosaurs because it had this really cool exploding volcano on the cover and started with D-I. *Wrong.* And then, of course, her conversion to Catholicism when she was in her midsixties.

What's weird is that I don't remember her ever talking about "battling" or struggling with Buddhism or New Age beliefs. And even in Catholicism, it was never a *battle*, though she did mention taking issue with some of the church's positions. Apparently, it was only the influence or threat of atheism in her heart that she felt she had to fight.

When she told me she was going to become a Catholic—"join the church" were her exact words—she actually seemed a little embarrassed in front of me. I think partly because *Jim & Casper Go to Church* was already out by then, so I was "out" as an atheist and all that. And wouldn't an atheist look down his nose even more on Catholicism, that most staid and established form of Christianity?

But it was probably more because we both knew the Catholic Church's position on homosexuality, women in positions of power, and so on. We both knew there were some fundamental positions in her new faith that would be anything but fundamental to our otherwise compatible world outlook (and she was pretty open about not being on board with most of the church's more conservative opinions).

But I was glad she was joining the church, even if it meant she had to become a Catholic. Her conversion didn't mean her doubts and spiritual struggles were over, by any means; that much was pretty clear. But embracing Catholicism meant—at least from my perspective—that she now had a framework within which to experience her struggles, which I think can be helpful.

It was always my mother's way to try things in the most complete way possible. For example, when she got into meditation, she didn't just meditate for an hour, she went on weeklong meditation retreats. I didn't think Catholicism would necessarily be her last stop. But as it turns out, it was.

I do think it was a good place for her mind to be when she got sick—this faith, this church, these people—because I think for her it was more about the people than the promise of heaven. (Although some of the people I met then were very much about the promise of heaven.)

Anyway, I could see how it bolstered her in almost every way. I think she took comfort in the various rituals and the history of it all. Not to mention the steadfastness of her Catholic compatriots who visited her bedside. There was no wavering, just prayer, Eucharist, prayer. It was always calming.

And though she knew I didn't believe in the foundations of her chosen faith for myself, I didn't dismiss the value she attributed to it either. I think that's why when I told her I was writing a book as an atheist, she was proud of me. Not because I was saying I had no faith, but because it was clear I didn't take this stuff—meaning faith, religious institutions, higher powers, and all—lightly. And then she liked the fact that I said I was *currently* an atheist. I think she felt that she had raised her son to be what she herself was above all else: a *seeker*.

JIM: Ah, *seekers* . . . another word I love. In the old days, we Christians also called them "lost" or even more effectively, "*the* lost." *Seeker* is a friendlier word than *lost*. It makes room for people who are looking for something—which we hope will be Jesus—but just haven't found it yet.

Jesus did not give admonishment or instruction about all aspects of our spiritual lives, but the one in Matthew 7 about seeking is probably one of the most important, because it not only challenges us to be seekers—to not be afraid to ask questions and to look for answers—it also promises a pretty big payoff if we do: We will find what we are looking for.

For many Christians, there is something really uncomfortable about questions. We're afraid to ask them for fear of getting an answer we can't reconcile. Or we shy away from questions for fear of not being able to offer "the right answer." Yet Jesus set the example for us. He was always inquiring. Several times, for example, He questioned Peter's love for Him, and He wasn't just being rhetorical. He asked His disciples, "Who do men say that I am?" looking for some indication of how the message was getting out. And in probably His most controversial and brazen question, He asked God, "Why have you forsaken me?" (Matthew 27:46).

If we learn anything from how Jesus operated, it is that we are *invited* to ask questions. God wants us to ponder our faith deeply. He wants us to consider fully, and weigh out diligently, what it means to commit to a life of following Him. He doesn't want us to simply embrace a religion because we inherited it, or to adopt faith on a whim. In her book *Called to Question*, Sister Joan Chittister explains, "It is God that religion must be about, not itself. When religion makes itself God, it ceases to be religion. But when religion becomes the bridge that leads to God, it stretches us to live to the limits of human possibility."[14]

I think of Casper's mother and how she went all-in, no matter where her seeking led her. Being unafraid to fully explore and fully question what it means to believe is the only way to get at the heart of the journey. It is the best way to be like Jesus.

Getting back to our trip to Boulder . . . the Young Life campus group we were meeting with was led by John and Marty Nunez. After talking with John and Marty for a few minutes, it became clear they themselves were still searching for something beyond standard-fare evangelicalism. This might explain why they welcomed us with open arms. I definitely thought of them as Christians, but my atheist colleague was picking up on something as well.

CASPER: I think I might put the Nunezes in the "seeker" category, too, though maybe not in the same way my mom was. Though I felt that John and Marty were seeking, it was definitely within the borders of their own faith. But their willingness to open themselves to Jim and me led me to believe at the time that they were looking for something more. I mean, they felt okay inviting an outsider—an atheist, no less—into their comfort zone, even if it meant their comfort zone might change—and maybe even no longer be all that comfortable.

I definitely remember being nervous. Here I was, an open atheist, coming into their house, as it were, and getting ready to be eviscerated. Based on the conversations I'd had with some of the radio callers, I was basically preparing my "thank yous" for all the people who would tell me I was going to hell. After all, my mother was in the room and the last thing I wanted was for her to see her son act ungraciously under pressure.

What we got that night, mostly, were people who simply were curious—people who had read the book and had come to the event with their curiosity piqued about atheism and about us. I certainly felt as if I were being examined. It dawned on me that I may very well be the first atheist these kids had ever met, let alone could ask questions of in a safe environment. When I realized they were there to learn, I felt a renewed sense of purpose.

For these college kids, unlike some of the folks we met during our radio interviews, meeting me didn't seem to threaten their faith. They seemed to understand that asking questions about someone else's belief system can often help us better understand our own beliefs, and even make our beliefs stronger.

JIM: The next morning, Casper and I spoke at Urban Skye, which, according to their website, is "a curious network of catalysts and communities joined in a common search for meaning." Their meeting hall was in an enormous former synagogue, which appeared to please Casper.

CASPER: Though they may have positioned themselves as "a curious network of etc., etc.," I pretty much saw a church service taking place in an old synagogue. The irony is not lost on me. The fact that it is well kept but no longer filled with Jews, but with Christians—it's like the conversion of Denver's Jews must have happened within a few recent months or something. Or maybe they all just moved away.

At any rate, this group was also receptive. They listened to our conversation and then, after asking me if it was okay, prayed for my soul. Similarly, many other folks we have met along the way—Catholics, Baptists, Methodists, and more—have told me that they would pray for me. The difference was that this group of people in Colorado actually asked me first.

This came off as a pretty strange question to me. I blinked my eyes in astonishment the first couple of times. I have no correlation for this. The closest thing I can say, as a current nonpray-er, would be something like, "Would it be okay with you if I fondly remember you and our conversation here today?" So of course it's okay, but I always qualified my response: "I am A-okay with your praying for me, provided you're not praying for me to get hit by a bus."

The people in Denver who wanted to pray for me weren't taking the "grab hands, say it out loud" approach. They were simply showing respect for me and my beliefs, and I appreciated that (though I do wonder, if I had said, "No, don't pray for me," if they would have gone ahead and done so anyway . . . gotta figure). But when I think about it—which I often do—even though I may not believe there is a God listening to their prayers, it seems silly that I would have a problem with anyone thinking or saying basically kind and hopeful things about me.

JIM: Following our event at Urban Skye, we went to The Refuge, an outdoor church event near Denver, hosted by Kathy Escobar and Karl Wheeler. From a distance, it had a Great Gatsby kind of feel—white tents, green lawn—at least that was my impression. Casper thought it looked like a revival meeting at a golf club.

By the time we got to The Refuge, we were beginning to figure out our shtick. We'd show up, give some background on how we got together for this unusual project, read the first few pages of the Saddleback chapter from *Jim & Casper* in our own voices (with some dramatic flair added, of course), and then open up the floor for comments and questions. It wasn't unusual to get a mixture of statements, including, "Casper, you're going to hell," and, "Jim, why aren't you saving Casper from going to hell?"

This was indicative of the challenge we faced along the way, and it was not really the kind of questioning I think Jesus would have brought to us. We had hoped to open up the conversation so the Christians we were encountering would begin to ask thoughtful questions of us and of themselves. Questions such as, "Casper, what are your biggest objections to a life of faith?" or "Jim, what have you learned in your experience with Casper that can help us be more effective in sharing our faith with nonbelievers?"

Maybe that was a bit too much to expect on this initial venture, but that's why we're now writing this book. We hope to show that questioning—whether internal, with fellow Christians, with people who don't share your faith, or aimed directly at God—when done in a spirit of truly seeking understanding, is one of the greatest ways to grow in faith.

CASPER: I remember a guy at The Refuge standing up and asking if Jim had adequately explained the gospel to me. And

I remember Jim's response being along the lines of, "Casper knows our offer."

That took me aback. I don't remember thinking of it as an *offer* before. And I wondered . . . *had* Jim adequately explained the gospel to me? What comprises *adequate*? I had some doubts: Even though I had four years at a Catholic college and had attended literally dozens of churches . . . was it possible that the gospel had not been adequately explained to me? Had I missed something?

JIM: To clarify, the gospel this man wanted Casper to understand more clearly—what he feared I might have failed to explain— was this: Accept Christ and you go to heaven; reject Him and you go to hell.

The gospel (as I see it) is this: Jesus likes human beings so much He became one. Here's what I mean: Jesus entered our world as the Servant who also happened to be the Savior. We've made the mistake of separating the two and giving precedence to one over the other. Jesus is clearly the Savior, but that act of redemption sits inside His humanity. There are at least five major theories on atonement and what exactly that act did for us. These differing viewpoints are the types of disagreements that create new doctrines and keep believers divided.

We have questions swirling around about our origins, questions attempting to unravel the confusion about salvation, questions about the unfolding of Christ's return. But we have really zeroed in on the wrong things to question. They are the least relevant of any of the ponderings on which we could spend our time. The better questions address how we are supposed to live, how we should treat one another, and how we can get closer to knowing God and what He wants for our lives. They are questions of relationship and communication. They are also proof that not all questions must lead to an argument. Jesus' solidarity with people shines through.

CASPER: One significant thing that really stands out about this particular leg of our journey is a young woman who took a very active interest in me and my mom. Maybe it was the Christian "respect your elders" thing, but she just seemed genuinely interested and caring, without any kind of agenda.

Of course, professional me—marketing me—saw it a little differently at first, thinking, *What's her angle here?* But it turns out she was just following her heart, and—as she told me—her heart belonged to God in many ways.

This was kind of an "aha" moment for me. Granted, she had read our book and was there to hear us speak, but her behavior was all about simply caring. And it was driven by her faith, which, as far as I could tell, simply said "care about others." It was a pretty big deal to me then and remains so now, perhaps because she was caring for others without caring about whether or not it was seen or had to be seen at all.

It's moments like those that I find the most impactful— when someone cares for someone else and needs no credit or recognition. I mean, you don't need a bunch of T-shirts to proclaim, "I participated in Clean up a Poor Neighborhood Day, 2013." You just need to clean up the neighborhood. If anyone notices or gives you an "Atta boy!" well, that's just frosting on the cake.

JIM: Casper's observation about the young woman in Boulder who chose not to draw attention to herself cuts to the heart of what I'm trying to communicate about the Christian life. While questioning and seeking help us grow, there is one simple truth we should never question: *Jesus called us to serve.* As Joan Chittister says, "We must not, if we are to be spiritual people, fail to realize that life is meant to be nothing but a growing ground in God. If we fail to cultivate that part of us that is our truest self, how can the self come to full life in us? The spiritual life is the discovery of the self God meant us to be so that who we are can be God's gift to the rest of the world."[15]

I believe this young woman who had such an impact on Casper was exemplifying this principle. She was exemplifying Jesus, God's greatest gift to the world.

IT'S ALL OVER *INCLUDING* THE SHOUTIN'

JIM: You've probably heard the old saying, "It's all over but the shoutin'." We often toss around clichés without really understanding what they mean. This one is most commonly understood to mean that the deal is done. It's all but settled. However, within the nuance of that statement is a wide opening for communication to break down. The shoutin' part means that, though the outcome is known, there still remain some details to hash out . . . and we all know the devil is in the details.

The point is, the shouting match that can come with settling the ins and outs of an issue is typically when common ground is lost and where civility leaves the premises. The following discussion takes on this challenge of finding points we can all agree on and figuring out where to concede, where to agree to disagree, and where to compromise for the sake of the relationship and an honest exchange of ideas.

CASPER: As Jim and I went along this journey of writing the first book and spending time talking to all these Christians, my mother had a somewhat startling insight into how the experience had affected me. She knew where I was in my life—or my search, if you prefer—and she knew that there was no point in asking whether any of this had changed my mind about God. She knew that pestering a nonbeliever like me about "when" I might come to Christ is pretty much a nonstarter. I think people need to address the *why* before the *when*.

Anyway, one day she said, "I think all of this has made you more tolerant." And my response was along the lines of, "I have to be, Mom. Being intolerant of a belief just because I don't share it . . . I mean, what's the point? Even if I wanted to somehow 'win people over' to being nonbelievers, well, I'm not going to change anyone's mind by getting in their face. And in most cases, I'm not sure I would even want to change anyone's mind."

To me, the meaning of *tolerance* is suspending judgment first and foremost and being willing to listen with an open mind. It's the "willing to listen" part that is central to the concept because the act of being tolerant starts with understanding that people have a basic need to be heard. To show tolerance, we really need to be quiet first. This can be especially challenging in the context of deeply held beliefs. It's like, "Of course I tolerate your views! But I would rather express mine!"

Usually when we have a strong desire to share a thought, belief, or opinion, we forget the fundamental principle of tolerance and tend to *tell* others this and *tell* them that, and we focus on trying to convince the other person to agree—mainly by not letting him or her get a word in edgewise. Failing that, we begin to shout, as if that will help convey the message more clearly.

I think part of my definition of *tolerance* comes from my mother's perspective on my "improved tolerance." I knew I *felt* that way, but I couldn't quite put my finger on the reason. She said I was more open-minded and a better listener than I used to be. I think that was all a part of focusing on *dialogue* rather than *debate*, which admittedly was kind of new for me. It wasn't that I didn't dialogue before all of this, but I also didn't shy away from an opportunity to show off—verbally, that is. Nothing fired me up more than, say, an argument about politics, or music, or food . . . or an argument about *anything*, really. Including God.

The Casper of about ten years ago—before meeting Jim and writing the first book—would get fired up about anything, and would likely be arguing right now, throwing all kinds of "black-and-white" facts around, talking fast, talking loud, focusing on my target like a lawyer, and listening only long enough to spot an opportunity to say "Aha!!!"

I think about my college years, when I was not all that interested in what anyone who disagreed with me had to say. I had *the facts*, I knew *what was going on*, and if you disagreed with me, it wasn't because you had facts I hadn't learned yet—after all, I had *the* facts—or that your life experience had led you to see some facts differently; it was because you were *wrong*.

But as my mom noticed, I had changed.

I think I got tired of fighting. I mean, I was the go-to guy for debating anything. I've considered the possibility that it's because I'm a dad now, but that's not really it because I was arguing plenty after my kids were born. I can remember when my daughter Evelyn was one or two and I was arguing with strangers on my morning commute about why invading Iraq was un-American. (Yes, I was *that guy*.) So the best reason I came up with for being more tolerant is that I simply wanted to be more *effective* in my relationships with others.

JIM: Respect for the other person and the ideas he or she brings to the table is the first step in any constructive interaction. As missional theologian David Bosch says, "We cannot possibly dialogue with or witness to people if we resent their presence or the views they hold."[16] The desire to be more effective in relationships may sound like Self-Help Guru 101, but it is much more difficult to achieve than we anticipate. For one thing, we tend to have a narrow view of what constitutes a relationship. We think of family, friends, partners, and maybe even colleagues; but rarely do we consider that *every* interaction, regardless of how long it lasts, is the foundation of a relationship—because if we're doing it right, we are *relating* to the other person.

CASPER: Part of what has changed for me over the past few years is learning that life becomes infinitely more interesting when I *create connections* rather than clashing with people. It's easier than you think too. After all, everyone except a sociopath wants to make the world a better place. We may differ on what that means and how it is translated into action, but we have the same starting point.

I started thinking about what I could do to make the world a better place. And while some folks may be ready to make the world a better place by fighting poverty in the inner city or by jumping on a plane to help children on the other side of the world, I had to take a baby step and do a better job of working on connecting with people in my own backyard who differ with me. In America, we're surrounded by people with divergent beliefs and values, so there's opportunity everywhere.

Jim and I spend a lot of time independently with people

who approach faith in a manner not like our own—he likes his "lost" people and I like my "found" people—but I think most people shy away from such relationships. And it's a shame; because if all you do is spend time with people who think and believe the way you do, your chances of learning new things—about others, about yourself—diminish significantly.

Some friends of mine who are nonbelievers have asked me for intellectual ammunition they can use when they find themselves in arguments with Christians or other people of faith. They assume that because I'm an atheist who is often in the Christian space, I must be debating all the time and have my "anti-Christian" arguments dialed in.

They're always surprised—and I mean 100 percent of the time, without exception—when I tell them I don't have any anti-Christian arguments to make; that I think Christianity, as written, is a pretty positive thing. I tell my nonbelieving friends that I ask questions of Christians about the perceived positives and negatives of their faith and how they personally reconcile them. And I share with inquiring atheists that it makes for a lot more interesting and constructive conversation if we're working on seeing things from the other person's side. I tell them I would prefer to *ask questions* about a person's faith than insult it. It's far more constructive all around.

I'm not sure what Dale Carnegie would say about this way of "influencing" people, but I've come to believe that the best path to being more effective is to try to affect people less. I'm currently trying to *connect* with people more than *affect* them.

Of course, we—and by *we* I mean myself and most of the Christians I've met—have entirely different views on the matters that connect us, as we're usually talking about faith. But I don't feel the need to "convert them" to my side because

I don't think there's anything all that terrible about believing in God. I don't think there's a "price to pay" for believing. Whereas they believe there is a hefty price to pay for *not* believing. I don't have an atheistic alternative for eternal damnation. There is none. And I'm glad, because that would be just another stumbling block for us. Can you imagine how that would go?

Them: You're going to the Christian version of hell.

Me: You're going to the atheist version of hell.

Them: You're going to the Christian version of hell—twice!

Me: You're going to the atheist version of hell—*three* times, and no givebacks!

So while I understand my Christian friends' concerns, most of them understand I don't share those concerns. I believe they have decided to be friends with me anyway, rather than just giving me up for damned and walking away. (Who knows? Maybe that will create opportunities to save me!)

It's usually the people who know me the least who think I need to be saved the most, which is kind of weird, when you think about it. Many of the people who would try to "save me" never really take the time to know me. Maybe saving me would be a terrible idea! Maybe I'm the one guy who will make heaven a boring, miserable place for others. . . . I can see it now, a bunch of sulky angels: "Heaven used to be cool . . . until *he* got here. . . . Now it's totally lame."

And what happens when you convert someone anyway? I think one thing that happens is you risk eliminating the one thing that makes them different from you. And, yes, you're left with one less difference, but maybe it's the one difference that makes all the difference.

Maybe that's why I never, ever try to "convert" anyone to atheism in our many talks and speaking engagements and the like. I don't try to get them over to whatever "my side" is, nor do I look for holes in their reasoning, or focus on spotting chinks in the armor so I can land a blow. I think I'd rather learn something, so I just listen. I wish it worked both ways, but sometimes in these discussions, listening becomes a one-way street. Sometimes, the people who want to save me simply want me to hear what they think, to hear their story. But to succeed at listening (which is part of succeeding at dialogue), we must try as hard as we can to put ourselves in the other person's shoes—both when we're listening and when we're speaking. This approach usually leads to more questions than anything else.

When I'm talking to people, I try to imagine the context of their lives. *This isn't* nobody *I'm talking to*, I remind myself. *This is* somebody, *who probably sees me in much the same way as I see him or her—and that means neither of us is more important than the other, nor is what we have to say more or less important.*

People who stink at dialogue are typically those who are overly self-involved. Most people would say we talk *to* someone; but if we're dialoguing—going back and forth—it's really *with* someone. What a difference a preposition makes. And if you're with someone, I think you should focus on the *with*.

JIM: I don't think anyone would disagree with Casper here, but it's still very easy to choose debate over *dialogue*. We can "listen with our imagination," and we can be *with* the person we're speaking to and yet still be as rigid as ever when it comes to matters of faith. Perhaps in part because this is a topic that is so subjective and so personal, we cling more tightly to our positions and fight more aggressively for them. After all, what good is a belief that we don't defend with conviction?

But I believe we are far more likely to have meaningful dialogue, and we stand a greater chance of influencing the way other people think, when we balance our passion with perspective, when we temper our tempers, tame our tongues, and allow for the kind of engaged listening that Casper describes.

Remember Jesus' interaction with the woman at the well? He of all people could have pounded His chest and demanded that she acknowledge Him as the Messiah and accept Him as her Savior. By some measure, He would have been justified. Instead, He laid out the information for her to receive and do with as she saw fit, in her own timing. Once again, we see that Jesus showed us how to get it done. He demonstrated that patience and tolerance, which are in all of us, are the most effective communication tools.

CASPER: When I think back to what my mom said about my being more tolerant, I know now, and knew then, that being tolerant didn't just happen for me. I chose it. When I found myself thrust into new environments—churches and other Christian gatherings—filled with people very different from me, it was my mission to *learn*. (After all, I had a book to write!) I think when we truly want to learn, we listen as much as possible and speak as little as possible. And when we speak, it's not to give our opinion but to ask questions so we can learn even more.

Here's the thing: I know I'm relatively smart. But that knowledge served me poorly for a long time because there's a fine line between being "pretty smart" and being a know-it-all. And for years, I was basically a know-it-all. Being a know-it-all gives us confidence in many ways. But I don't think it's the right kind of confidence. I think it's an ego driven sense of unwavering certainty, and certainty can be more harmful than helpful. It can render us unable to learn new things—because why would we need to learn something new when we know it all already? Being certain really means being a know-it-all, in the end. And I didn't want to be that.

It wasn't until I realized that I might not be as smart as I thought I was that I became a better listener, a better learner, a better dialoguer, and (as my mom saw) a more tolerant person.

JIM: Leonardo Da Vinci reportedly said, "Where there is shouting there is no true knowledge."[17] I think many people today are under the mistaken impression that a shortage of facts can be concealed by an escalation of volume. A shouting match, even among people of intelligence, yields nothing in the exchange of ideas. It's impossible to learn from anyone when all the useful stuff is drowned out by vitriol.

I love what Stephen Prothero says on the topic: "Virtue needs a neighbor."[18] For me, learning to listen to atheists and other people who don't believe what I believe has helped me practice virtue.

CASPER: I agree completely that virtue needs a neighbor. In most conversations, there's an opportunity to learn something new about someone else, discover something new about ourselves, or simply practice virtuous behavior. For example, I remember a party after one of our speaking events. This fella kind of backed me into a corner and began yelling at me about how I "didn't get it." Ten years ago, I would have been yelling right back, "No, *you* don't get it, pal," or something equally childish. Instead, I tried focusing on how he felt about what he was saying. (I couldn't quite get there because . . . well, he was yelling.) But I saw this as an opportunity to practice patience—a virtuous behavior.

I wasn't successful in getting him to stop attacking me,

but I did avoid attacking him back. Eventually, a friend of his saw what was going on and diplomatically escorted his yelling Christian friend away. Though I prefer a dialogue to a debate, sometimes all we can do (or hope for someone else to do) is put out the fire.

JIM: It doesn't do the Christian message or community any good to have attack dogs who create a hostile environment for outsiders. We don't need guards at the gate. We need a welcoming committee. But hostile attacks are what happen when we choose to speak without listening and try to convert without caring.

Christians in America have a tendency to assume that the majority is aligned with us and to treat as foreign anyone who is not a part of us. The United States has historically been thought of as a Christian nation. In fact, our Congress, which in recent times has been unable to agree on much of anything, suddenly discovered the collective will to reaffirm our nation's motto, *In God We Trust*.

Though much could be said about the irony of that motto, I am curious to know what it feels like to be an atheist in a supposedly Christian nation. How does our national motto square with the image of a yelling Christian? How does this motto affect a nonbeliever's connection to his or her country or national identity? Do people of differing faiths, or no faith at all, feel excluded by such an attachment to a specific belief system?

CASPER: Sometimes I take solace in the fact that we live in what I think Jim rightfully calls a *supposedly* Christian nation. If our country were really all about following the teachings of Jesus Christ, then I would be endlessly grateful because that would mean the 80 percent of Americans who call themselves Christians were putting the needs of others ahead of their own. With odds like that, we can't help but be a great country.

But we all know that's not the case. Within only a few miles—and in some cases, only a few blocks—of every mega-church Jim and I visited, we can safely assume there were homeless people, families without enough to eat, and suffering of almost every kind.

And when it comes to how my supposedly Christian nation deals with other nations . . . well, let's just say it's hard to imagine Jesus being okay with the number of deadly weapons this Christian nation and its people have and use, not to mention the amount of warfare this country engages in.

Christians supposedly base all they believe on the Bible and the words of Jesus, but man, a lot has changed since 0 AD. And the Bible is filled with contradictions, too. I mean, we all know that Jesus commanded His followers to take care of the needy and the poor, yet there are passages in the Bible that appear to condone, or at least not condemn, slavery. Come on, now! Maybe I haven't done enough digging here, but who is more needy or poor than someone who is enslaved?

And let me take a look at the log in my own eye with this irony: Many atheists get up in arms over fundamentalism, which I translate as people taking the Bible literally. However, we—well, at least I—also expect people to take the words of Jesus literally. We would rather that Christians not strictly apply the hateful words in Leviticus or the words of Paul, who, based on what little I know, was one of the people who gave the thumbs-up to slavery. It's like we atheists want you to dismiss much of the Old Testament as antiquated or allegorical, and yet we expect you to take the words of Jesus as . . . umm . . . gospel. Well, the stuff we agree with, anyway.

So when you ask me about the incongruities foisted upon

me living in a supposedly Christian nation where folks don't practice all that much Christian charity . . . I think I'd say we're pretty much on the same page. We all have to live with inconsistencies: in our nation, in our belief systems, in our friends, families, and selves. I think if we're unable to accept the fact that life on every level is filled with contradictions, we'll go crazy. I think that's why Jim and I get along so well; we're both aware of and okay with the conundrum.

That's also why dialogue is more productive and ultimately more satisfying, than debate. Debate focuses on finding the contradictions in the other person's argument—and then pouncing on them. But when we're focused on dialogue instead of debate, we accept contradictions as unavoidable.

I know Jim wants to save me from hell, and we both know I don't believe hell is real; but we accept this incongruity. And maybe we even go one better. I think it's the contradictions that bind us together because they give us endless things to talk about. I rather enjoy being in the company of someone who sees the world in a radically different way than I do.

JIM: The ability to hold on to two opposing ideas at the same time—a.k.a. *contradictions*—is a challenge for the best of us. It brings us back to the fear that questioning exposes weakness and that opening our minds to consider another perspective threatens the security of our faith. While this might be true in some cases, the only way to really know that our faith is sound is by having it tested and being able to share it without fear of what opposition we might encounter. "As iron sharpens iron, so one person sharpens another" (Proverbs 27:17). It is another clear message that we are supposed to use one another, engage in dialogue, and listen and hear other perspectives so we can become sharper in our own faith.

WHEN BAD THINGS HAPPEN
TO DAMNED PEOPLE

JIM: As you know, Casper's mother lost her battle with cancer during the course of the work he and I did together. There has been so much focus on understanding why Casper doesn't believe what he doesn't believe and how we might change his mind. But we haven't really looked at what he does believe and what framework he operates in for dealing with life's biggest questions and challenges—the kind that are never more relevant than when someone we love leaves this life to answer once and for all what happens after we die. I'm going to turn most of this chapter over to Casper to share what he experienced, the impact it has had on him and his perspective on Christianity or faith of any kind, and whether or not this loss has made a difference in how he believes.

CASPER: When we got the diagnosis in April 2007, that's when the clock started ticking on my mom's life. In August 2007, she started chemo. By November, she was in remission. In January 2008, she had a relapse. By June 2008, she was gone.

We all know about death, and someday we'll all get the chance to experience it firsthand. But unlike the way I just accounted for the events and times of my mom's illness, her death was more a journey of emotions than a chronology of dates. And like most folks, I was familiar with the five stages of that journey: denial, anger, bargaining, depression, acceptance.

I know what my friends from various religions say: Death is the start of something new—it's when we join God (Christians), or when we go to sleep until angels reawaken us (Islam), or when we have the chance to be reincarnated as anything from a bug to a dog to a deity (Hinduism).

For me, it's not the start of anything. I see it more as the completion of a transaction begun when we were born. Death is the price we pay for living. A fact, plain and simple. That's how I see it. And it's not just our own deaths—it's any death. Being in denial of death or living in fear of death is like going swimming and refusing to think you'll get wet or being afraid of getting wet. Getting wet is part of going swimming. It's unavoidable and intrinsic.

And though I think no one can feel happy about death— our own, those of our loved ones, or even the death of a stranger—most of the emotions (happiness, sadness, denial, anger, bargaining, depression) don't figure much into my understanding. The last of Elisabeth Kubler-Ross's stages— *acceptance*—is where I would choose to bide my time. At least it was when my mom was dying.

Toward the end, I visited her and sat by her side, accepting that each time might be the last. And she seemed to know and accept this too. We would smile through our tears when it was time for me to leave her bedside in Colorado to fly back to San Diego.

"See you next weekend, okay, Mom?"

She would nod and say something like, "I'm planning on it." We both hoped to see each other the following weekend, but we both accepted that it might not happen.

In the end, I got the phone call on a Thursday morning, flew there immediately, and was right by her side when she died that evening.

She actually waited for me. The last words anyone heard her say were, "When will Matthew be here?" They told her it would take about eight hours. Eight hours later, I showed up, let her know I was there, sat by her side, and she died about ten minutes later. That was it. She was gone. There was no more fear, no more worrying, no more anything, really. It was exactly as if a light had gone off. And I immediately accepted the fact that the light would not come back on.

Acceptance made it easier. I'm not saying there wasn't sadness, and there weren't tears. There was and there still are. But I peacefully accept the fact that I will never see my mom again. And when I die, well, that'll be it for me, too.

When I talk to Christians about death, the first question they invariably ask is, "What do you think happens after you die?" And I invariably say, "The same thing that happened before you were born. Which is to say, nothing." The way I see it, we're a little blip on a time line that goes on infinitely in each direction. Most everyone sweats what will happen *after* their own blip, but not so much what happened before it. The way I see it, there's very little difference. I know that is a hard thing for anyone to accept—myself included; we can't really fathom this time line because we see so little of it.

Lately, I've been wondering about the dread we all have of dying. I don't deny that I'm pretty sure I dread death, just like everyone. But dread is different from fear. Fear, to me, means being afraid of something unknown. Dread is . . . well, I think the word conveys a sense of resignation, which is just another word for acceptance, when you think about it.

I think this dread is something we all share, no matter what we believe, because no one wants to die, really. We spend so much money and time doing all we can to preserve and prolong life. But I wonder about the nature of this dread: Do we dread death itself—the unknown, the unfathomable—or do we dread not being alive?

I'm beginning to think that I don't dread death itself. Death itself happens in an instant, after all. Dying may take time, but death comes in the blink of an eye. I think Hollywood has given us plenty of visions of what dying is like: a final big breath, a slight startle as a look of shock/awakening/insight/cosmic understanding/dread crosses the person's face, eyes briefly flare open wide, then a collapse into breathless silence, eyes closed, head lolled . . . roll credits.

Trying to imagine the world and our friends and families going on without us (somehow! some way! struggling!) is where I think our troubles really begin; because when we die, the world—for us as touching, tasting, hearing, feeling creatures—ends. Period. Right? I think we can all agree on that because whether we go on to nothing or on to something else, we are no longer experiencing this world as living beings.

But this "end of experience," with the world somehow getting along without us . . . well, that's what was happening before we were born. The world was humming right along . . . just as it will be after we're gone. And yet we don't dread or live in agony over all we missed before we were born. I think it's only because we've had a taste of life that we agonize over not having more. Our appetite for life is endless, which is why the dread of death is so pervasive.

So this "end of experience" is really only the end of our personal experience. Once we've lived, we're always alive. We leave our mark—the things we did, the words we said, the impressions we made all have a ripple effect while we're alive that continues after we're gone. We live on in how what we said and did affected others.

By that token, it's easy for me to say that Jesus is very much alive today, as His words and deeds continue to impact others in tremendous ways. It's easy for me to say that John Lennon is alive too. As is the father whose children live their lives according to how he raised them. As is my mom.

So do I believe in eternal life? Yes, I do. Sort of. But unlike my Christian friends, this "eternal life" is not one I experience in person in heaven, or when I'm resurrected by the Messiah's returning, or taken by angels sent from Allah. I believe life is eternal—not my own personal life, but a historical, collective life, if you will. As I was a part of this whole living thing—though ever so briefly—I am a part of it eternally. My ripple continues to spread.

That's my intellectual take on death, what it means to me when I think about it. Intellectually, my mom's death was only an event, a moment: 2:10 a.m., June 20, 2008. But I *feel* about it too. My emotional take on her death is something else entirely. Her being gone? It's as if I've lost part of my sight. I look around and I just can't see as much or as well as I once could. When you lose someone close—whether you believe in an afterlife or not—life is just not the same. And while I accept that, it doesn't mean it feels good. Accepting something like death often means accepting the missing pieces and the pain that comes with them too.

Though my mom is almost as alive in my heart and in my thoughts as she was when I could call her up and talk with her, I would give almost anything to actually talk with her again. All I do now is talk *to* her, which isn't the same as talking *with* her because she doesn't answer back. But it's something. My mom's life and living—and the dying that *had* to come with it—continue to shape me.

That's the closest I come to eternal life: what she gave to me, I give to the people in my life; what I give to them, they give to others, ad infinitum. Talking with Christians, though, I know their view of eternal life is radically different. Eternal life is a personal thing: It's *you* and *me* living forever. I know that's pretty much what a lot of Christians have been trained to proclaim when they talk to people about God. And I get it. I mean, isn't that why Jesus died? Isn't the main point of sharing about His existence and His dying about getting people to heaven? Didn't Paul say that if Christ has not been raised from the dead then Christianity itself is . . . well . . . pointless?

JIM: Yes, Paul (whom some Christians call *Saint* Paul) did say that. And yes, I personally believe that Jesus physically rose from the dead and now sits at the right hand of God, where He will judge the living and the dead. But (and this is an important *but*) that doesn't mean getting to heaven or staying out of hell is supposed to be The Story we tell people. As our good friend Todd Hunter says, "Heaven is not the *goal*; it's the destination."[19] The goal is spiritual transformation into Christlikeness—which means that if Casper is right and this whole thing is a figment of our collective imaginations, or if John Lennon was right when he said there's "no hell below us, above us only sky,"[20] people who follow Jesus will still have experienced transformation by attempting to walk in the steps we read about in the Gospels.

Nevertheless, though Christians love to talk and sing about the glories of heaven, when it's our turn to die, we often appear to resist it as intensely as if we were headed for hell. We think about heaven, but as a group we have a long way to go when it comes to doing what Jesus told us to do, which was pray that His Kingdom would come on earth as it is in heaven (see Matthew 6:10). Yet, apart from attending church, most of our time on earth is spent doing pretty much what people who don't care about heaven do: watching too much TV, eating too much food, and consuming too much in general.

We are content to go about our daily lives generally unaffected by death and what comes after. In fact, we are able to eventually move past loss, consoling ourselves in the thought that our loved ones are with God. That is a great comfort for believers. But is there comfort to be derived by the nonbeliever when their believing friends or family pass? So I asked Casper if it bothered him, philosophically, that she could be in heaven right now, since she was Catholic and believed in such a place.

CASPER: Hey, if heaven is real, then I hope she is there. And I'm glad you brought up my mom's faith, because it was the people who led her to her faith—the people in her church— who made her dying more bearable. Not so much through what they said to us, but what they did for us . . . especially the Flanagans. They're a family at my mom's church (Christ the King in Evergreen, Colorado) who opened their home to my mother and to me, my sister, the whole family.

Originally, they were going to provide my mother with a place to recover from a marrow transplant. Yvonne Flanagan is a nurse, and they had extra rooms in their house. My mom was scheduled to get a transplant when she was in remission, but she didn't stay in remission long enough. So the Flanagans made a choice—and as far as I could tell, didn't hesitate one moment—to change their house from a place of recovery to a hospice. The Flanagan kids had grown up and left home a few years back, so there were enough beds for me, my sister, and other visitors, a place where my mother could have a room and bathroom of her own. They made their home into a safe haven and a place of comfort for people who were essentially strangers. My mom knew the Flanagans from church, of course, but it's a pretty big church. I met a few people from the church during previous visits, but the first time I met the Flanagans was when I went to visit my dying mother in their home. I am forever grateful, and that level of kindness is impossible to repay.

The kindness came from the whole church community, too. Every time I visited, I was usually one of many at her bedside. Her friends would pray with her every day, the priest would come and give her Communion, and I would be there, endlessly gratified for the comfort and support she received from those people and their prayers.

The only thing I ever struggled with was talk of heaven, especially after she died. Her friends and community knew what I believed—that there is no such thing as heaven—and yet some people told me things such as, "She's looking down on you right now." I knew they were saying the same kinds of things they'd say to anyone and only trying to make me feel better, but for some reason it made me feel worse. Perhaps it was because my mom's death, for me, was a time to celebrate her life and enjoy the gifts she had given us, not a time to talk about seeing her again.

I felt no need to openly reject what they were saying (I would only say "thank you"), but I think they were more accustomed to people agreeing, "Yes, she's in heaven." Heaven was presented as a fact, not as something that might not be a shared reality. That said, it wasn't an unbearable thing to hear either; it wasn't as if anyone was trying to leverage it or anything. No one said to me, "You know, if you became Catholic, you could see her again." I don't imagine I would have had a kind response for something like that.

These were just kind, caring people who were simply sharing what they truly believed: My mom was in heaven. I understood then and understand now that thinking of heaven is a great source of comfort for many people. And I had no interest in challenging anyone's right to their source of comfort.

My comfort was, instead, in my mom's life. And in her dying, my comfort was in the gift that the Flanagans and the entire community gave to me and my family, which was how my mother was allowed to die. She died in a safe, warm place, in the company of friends and family. I cannot think of a more gentle and connected way to die.

JIM: This is a beautiful example of everything Christians are supposed to do: They took care of someone who was suffering and expected nothing in return. And they prayed over her. It is in life's most trying times that people lean on God. They find great refuge in being able to unload concerns as well as gratitude through prayer. I asked Casper how he felt when his mother's friends prayed, or what he thought those friends might have felt about praying in front of him, an "out atheist."

CASPER: I don't believe there was any conscious concern on the part of these people about praying in the company of a guy they knew was an atheist (after all, my mother had made them all read *Jim & Casper Go to Church*—twice, probably). Maybe they just wanted me to witness the power of prayer, demonstrate how it supported them, show me what they leaned on, and without saying so directly, let me know that this support was available to me, too. Which I think is a warm and welcoming thing to do.

They weren't preaching; they were practicing. I think the last thing you should do in times of trouble or tragedy is to start preaching. When you preach at someone, you don't come to serve that person, but to serve up your own agenda. For me, when people are hurting and in need of healing, it is the absolute wrong time to focus on an agenda of conversion.

I remember talking to someone who had a prison ministry. We actually clashed about it. He said he was serving those most in need. I agreed, but I also mentioned that it could appear as if he were going after the "low-hanging fruit." He agreed with this at first, as he saw those people as the ones most in danger, those closest to falling off the tree, as it were.

However, I said it could also be interpreted as targeting the easiest pickings. He didn't care for this take on it. He made it clear that he in no way was going after them because they were vulnerable; he was trying to help people in trouble, people who were desperate. While I didn't want to beat up on the guy, I felt it was important to explain that, from an outsider's perspective, it could appear to be kind of opportunistic, like the way a lion will zero in on a young or lame wildebeest rather than a big, sturdy one. This got him more than a little mad, and I realized I should have found a better way to say what I was thinking.

But, based on what he told me, his way of helping the prisoners—"Choose Jesus and you will be saved"—would be more warmly welcomed by someone in dire straits.

I can't claim to know his motives beyond what he told me, of course; but when someone responds to a simple difference in perspective with such a defensive attitude, it is my educated guess that we're bumping up against an agenda that will come before anything else, one that must be protected at all costs, one that totally gets in the way of open conversation, and—in my opinion—the ability to form a connection with someone. This person is not interested in knowing me; he's only interested in presenting his agenda to me, in pitching me.

JIM: The truth is, we're almost always giving a pitch to someone, whether it's on a point of view, an opinion, a belief, a product, a service, or a political position. Even when we're doing something like discussing a movie we've seen, chances are we're either recommending it or criticizing it. It could be said that we all unavoidably navigate through life with an agenda. That doesn't have to be a bad thing. The "rightness" or "wrongness" of it rests entirely on how those agendas are presented and when.

CASPER: I think that's the nature of all communication: There's a certain subjectivity to everything we say. Even when I am doing something as fundamental as explaining how I feel, I'm kind of "pitching" myself to the other person so that he or she will understand where I'm coming from. To paraphrase a line I heard, "If you want to make God laugh, tell Him your agenda."

For me, the difference between a healthy, "agenda-free" dialogue and one that's more of a hard sell may depend on the self-awareness of the participants—do they realize their respective agendas, no matter how slight or incidental, and can they, in turn, share that awareness with the other person?

I think about the time I was in San Francisco with Jim and Julian (our partner in ChurchRater.com), and we talked about my mother's death as well as a situation that Julian was going through. As we offered up our stories of loss and struggle, some might say it was an ideal time for Jim to "witness" to us—you know, that if we had his faith, our struggles would not be something we had to carry alone, or some such message.

Instead, Jim listened to us and asked about how we felt. He didn't "leverage the opportunity." I don't believe a friend in need should ever be viewed as an opportunity. I know it may help some folks, when times are hard, to hear a litany on the blessings of Christianity; but to me, it would feel like ambulance chasing. Even if Christians mean well—offering what they see as helpful or even a possible salvation for a nonbeliever (like yours truly)—it could actually *come across* quite different, and cause the nonbeliever to stop feeling like a friend and start feeling like a target.

Even though I'm aware that Jim hopes I will someday come to Christ, I know he will not be relentless in pursuing that as an agenda, which leaves us free to have conversations that are as agenda free as possible. So as weird as it sounds, by not having an agenda to save me, Jim may have actually increased the chances for me to be saved.

In a similar way, I don't believe that any of my mother's Catholic friends were operating with an overt agenda. I think they just had hope—hope that she would recover, hope that her death would be peaceful, hope that her pain—and ours—would not be too great. That hope was something I could share with them.

If they had come at me with an agenda to save me or had used Christian conversion as some sort of if-then proposition—*You just lost your mom and you believe you'll never see her again, but if you convert, then you* will *get to see her again*—it would have been awful. But they did no such thing. They respected my beliefs, and they practiced theirs, and we found things we could share.

And though I may not have had the comfort of God at that time, I had the comfort of people who believe in God, and that made all the difference. When I look back, I think, *What glorious people*, and I find myself even hoping, for them, that what they believe is true because heaven is nothing less than what they deserve.

JIM: For Casper, losing his mother did not create a great revelatory conversion. It didn't make him run to the nearest altar to pray the "Sinner's Prayer." But his honest discussion of what he experienced holds some valuable lessons for everyone. First, for believers, it demonstrates the power of a loving, nonjudgmental approach to those in need of comfort, and the healing that prayerful support can offer to the most brokenhearted, no matter the status of their faith. For nonbelievers, it reveals the degree of comfort, solace, and encouragement that can come from the most unlikely sources when you are open to being cared for and accepting what comes from the purest of intentions.

IF ONE RELIGION DOESN'T WORK . . . CREATE ANOTHER

Both tolerance and respect are empty virtues until
we actually know something about whomever it is
we are supposed to be tolerating or respecting.
STEPHEN PROTHERO, *GOD IS NOT ONE*

JIM: When it comes to evangelism, Christians have been taught to appear friendly. This practice begins at church: When I say, "God is good," you're supposed to respond, "All the time." When it comes to how we are to act around nonbelievers, it can be even more contrived.

It's as if we Christians were *born again* lacking the gene that enables us to be *normal* around non-Christians. We're encouraged to take classes on how to develop "spiritual friendships," but if our new non-Christian friends fail to show sufficient interest in our beliefs or in our church, we're supposed to drop them as friends lest we slip down the ever-present slippery slope.

But here's what I've discovered through my friendship with Casper: Sometimes the proverbial slippery slope turns into something more like a *ski jump*—challenging, maybe even a little dangerous, but also something that can take us to new heights.

My relationship with Casper has pushed and prodded me in

directions I never anticipated. As I'm apt to say, "When people like each other, the rules change." Before I met Casper, I never sought to connect with atheists. I'm not really all that interested in atheism. I'm interested in *people*, some of whom happen to be atheists. In many ways, my relationships with nonbelievers may have saved my faith.

When we interact with people who disagree with us so profoundly about how reality is constructed, we have two choices: debate and leave or stay and dialogue. The thing that makes my relationship with Casper work is that we're equally committed to what I call "staying in the room." That means we don't walk away when we hit a philosophical impasse. Or at least we don't *stay* away; we might take a "time-out," but eventually we come back to continue our dialogue.

The fact that we are professionally (and I use that term very loosely) "stuck together" helps to motivate us; but frankly, there isn't enough money in this project to keep us going without some other motivating force at work. We stick together because we're both in love with an idea. Casper and I are curious. We want to know if people who are so different can really like each other; if they can have each other's back and defend each other behind each other's back.

That's part of what got me thinking about starting a new "religion."

I was pulled by my commitment to Casper and all the people I know who are different from me but whom I really like (sometimes even more than I like other Christians). Before you dismiss me completely, consider these questions:

- If Jesus came to twenty-first-century America, could He be a Christian?
- Would He want to?

- Which version of Christianity would He join?
- Where would He go to church?
- Would He need to take a "new believers" course in order to understand the religion that bears His name?
- When did Jesus express a desire to see His movement evolve into a world religion (and become the dominant one at that)?

Don't get me wrong: I'm still okay being called a Christian, even though I'm convinced Jesus could never be one. But like many, I've become increasingly uncomfortable with having to explain myself every time I admit that I'm a Christian.

Part of the reason I wrote this book is to help people (perhaps you) who have had this experience and are looking for a "Christianity-free" way to explain Jesus. It was my search for this freedom that led me to start a new "religion."

To use an analogy, Casper and I are both musicians. We've each spent years playing in a number of different bands. Here's how the music scene works: Sometimes guys will play in one band where they are famous and enjoy commercial success and then have a *side project* where they expand on the music they love and may explore things they wouldn't necessarily try with their "main band." Jack White of The White Stripes (and The Raconteurs, The Dead Weather, etc.) comes to mind, as well as Charlie Watts, drummer for The Rolling Stones, whose jazz projects (Charlie Watts and the Tentet, and the A, B, . . . of Boogie Woogie) allow the drummer to embrace his other affinities.

I'm like this with religion. Christianity is my main "religion," but I needed something else where I could experiment, explore, and stretch out spiritually. That's why I started practicing something I call *Otherlyness,* which is rooted in the life Jesus lived.

All their protestations notwithstanding, religions differentiate by one primary thing: *beliefs*. When it comes to religion, what you *believe* (in your head) far outweighs how you behave or what you put into practice. And yes, I include Christianity on this list.

Christianity has concerned itself far more with creedal orthodoxy than any other religion. This is in spite of the fact that what Jesus told us was important was what we *put into practice*—not whether Christ is actually or only symbolically present in the Communion bread or whether the Bible is infallible, literal, or a narrative. He did not ascribe nearly as much significance to the purity of the doctrinal information we carry around in our heads. In fact, doctrine didn't effectively exist until centuries after Jesus established the standard, when a bunch of guys got together to make rules about His teachings.

My work with Casper pushed me to confront these realities. As one of God's premier whistleblowers, Casper wouldn't let me off the hook. As someone with no vested interest in seeing Christianity retain its position as the largest religion in the world, Casper pressed me on its contradictions. And as someone who somehow got the impression (not sure where) that Christians were actually supposed to be *serving people who had needs*, Casper kept asking me why he wasn't hearing more about it in the church services we attended.

I ultimately came to the conclusion that when it comes to transforming human beings, beliefs are overrated. On their own, beliefs are incapable of changing a human heart. We have simply expected too much. The human experience is too complex for beliefs to profoundly influence us, which is why human beings say one thing and do another. The cable networks are rife with TV preachers who firmly believe what they preach but find it difficult to practice consistently. That's why it seems there's always somebody being caught in a sex scandal, investigated by the IRS for tax fraud, or outed by disillusioned congregants for abuses of power.

These harsh realities forced me to start a practice-centric and belief-free religion of sorts that even an atheist could join. While Otherlyness has no official *beliefs*, what it does have are three very important *practices*. You don't have to believe a thing to follow Otherlyness, but to call yourself a practitioner, you must *do something*, namely, these three practices:

1. I will be unusually interested in others, committed to asking questions and listening with the goal of learning.
2. I will "stay in the room" with differences, refusing to check out emotionally no matter how uncomfortable I may be.
3. I will stop comparing my best with your worst by first taking the proverbial log out of my own eye so that I can take an honest look at myself.[21]

That's it. If you do those three things—or even *try* to do them—you are by definition a practitioner of Otherlyness and a member of my religious side project, even if you have beliefs that are different from mine, or no beliefs at all.

Casper and I both try to practice these things. Otherlyness is the glue that holds us together. These practices provide us with an escape from the standard *us* vs. *them* paradigm. More and more, we tend to think of ourselves as simply an *us*.

That doesn't mean we never disagree, but it does mean we practice a radical kind of transparency. We still have our own agendas, but we *own* them. The odd part is that we've remained friends in spite of our differences. And it's not unique to the two of us. I've asked a number of nonbelievers if they find anything on this list of practices offensive, manipulative, sneaky, or contrived, and I have yet to hear anyone say yes.

I shared the three practices of Otherlyness with Ira Glass, the famous atheist public storyteller I mentioned earlier. He wrote them down as I recited them and then said, "I do those things."

I said, "I know you do, that's why you and I practice the same religion." He smiled and shrugged his shoulders, which I interpreted to mean he agreed with me (or was at least humoring me).

I no longer believe in "spiritual friendships," because as Danny DeVito's character in the must-see movie *The Big Kahuna* says, "As soon as you lay your hands on a conversation to steer it, it's not a conversation anymore—it's a pitch; and you're not a human being, you're a marketing rep."[22]

"Spiritual friendships" are a soft sell. They have a deeply hidden agenda. No matter how hard you try, you can't escape the grip of this agenda. Carl Meaderis, who wrote *Speaking of Jesus* and has worked with Muslims, decided not to evangelize anymore, but simply to talk *of* Jesus naturally and without an agenda. He has made a number of enemies inside Christianity for encouraging Muslims to stay Muslims and not become Christians, but to follow Jesus within Islam.

I began to wonder: *How can I remain faithful to this desire and commitment and not be a jerk who's "selling something"? How can I be normal and transparently follow Jesus, even in the face of disinterest or rejection? How can I be up-front and even proud (not arrogant) about what I think and feel about Jesus without becoming a person I don't like (pushy, insecure, and demanding)? How can I be a friend to people who don't hold my beliefs and are perhaps not interested at the moment in adopting them?*

These are the questions that naturally result from my relationship with Casper and other nonbelieving, or differently believing, friends I have made over the past fifteen years—friendships, by the way, that were made possible and that have grown wonderfully through my intentionally seeking satisfactory answers to these knotty questions.

My first opportunity to engage with these kinds of ideas came when I was invited to speak at the Secular Students Association at the University of Washington in 2008. They had heard about my work with atheists and became the first organization (Christian or non-Christian) to ask me to share my views and experiences.

Typical of Seattle, it was raining pretty hard as I made my way into the oversized classroom. It was after hours and this was a voluntary event. I was nervous because this was my first shot at speaking to a group of atheists.

"Before I start," I said, "I need to tell you guys what I *don't* do. I don't do arguments, and I don't care about creation disputes. I don't care about atheism. I'm too lazy to read the various arguments put forth by Richard Dawkins or James Dobson. I don't believe in religion, and I don't think you are stupid for not believing what I believe. Now what would you like to talk about?"

"Why do you follow Jesus?"

I thought it was a trick question (atheists can be smart that way), so I said, "You don't have to ask me that just to be polite."

"We aren't being polite, Jim, we're being curious. Seriously, why do you follow Jesus?"

As I stood there, I opened my heart and felt the presence of the Holy Spirit in the room. I was about to say something about it, but I realized how impolite and manipulative that would sound (let alone crazy) to a bunch of atheists. So I restrained myself and said, "I follow Jesus for one reason: He was the freest person who ever lived and I want to be free. That's why I follow Him."

Frankly, I had never articulated that idea before, but as I spoke those words, I knew they were true. I also realized that if I hadn't been constrained by the fact that I was talking with a roomful of nonbelievers, I would have fallen back into a less interesting way of expressing my followership of Jesus.

As I said earlier, some of the things we Christians have been taught, some of the ways our leaders have trained us, are pretty childish. One of the formative principles we've heard over and over is that people are more likely to respond to the gospel if we package it in a dramatic story. That's why people paint those dire pictures when they're trying to win another soul for the Lord. Facing a real live atheist is challenging, and maybe even emotionally disturbing, for people. They want to make a deep impression because these atheists aren't just *lost*—they're *super lost*.

This experience with atheists taught me the benefit of engaging with people I can't easily talk into my worldview. Removing the comfort of a shared vernacular forces us to think much more carefully about the terminology we select to express an idea. You can't fall back on the assumption that everyone is familiar with, much less agrees with, your dogma. This is what I mean when I say that working with Casper and other atheists saved my faith. I had to become deliberate in my faith and thoughtful in my expression of it. My aspirations of virtue needed a neighbor . . . and Casper signed up.

Casper is also a freedom junkie. The quest for personal freedom is a common denominator for us. My quest is inspired by the life of Jesus and energized (I believe) by His Spirit. Casper? Well, his quest currently gets its inspiration from somewhere else.

CASPER: Just like Jim, I want to live life as free as possible, and I don't mean free in the hedonistic sense. In my opinion, just pursuing one's desires is more like being enslaved than being free, and what's strange is that I have met more than a few people who have said that without their faith, they'd be doing God knows what—getting drunk all the time, stealing, and so on. I find it more than a little troubling that, for some folks, God appears to be nothing more than a hall monitor.

Based on some of the things people have said to me over the past few years, it sounds as if this country would be over-run with debauchery if we didn't have churches. I have actually heard someone say that without God, he would probably be raping and pillaging. I looked at his face to see if he was joking. Nope. So for some folks, I am absolutely thrilled they have found something to lean on or something to watch over them, both for the sake of their own well-being and that of others.

I mean, I'm glad you're not stealing my car or shooting heroin or taking advantage of other people . . . but lack-of-ethics-to-the-point-of-depravity is not the same thing as freedom.

To me, freedom is a state of mind. Look at Viktor Frankl, a Holocaust survivor and the author of *Man's Search for Meaning*. This guy found freedom in a Nazi concentration camp! He would not allow his situation or surroundings to poison his mind . . . he kept his mind free. I think that's what freedom is all about: feeling how you want to feel, saying what you want to say, expressing yourself no matter what—even if sometimes it's only to yourself.

JIM: While Casper and I are on the same page about the definition of freedom, I think how we pursue freedom may be a bit different. I choose Jesus as my model because I believe He was the freest person who ever lived. Choosing Jesus means that I have a clear path as to what kind of behavior is moral and what is hedonistic. Without God, or *a* god, to guide him, what helps Casper regulate the basic human tendency toward hedonistic impulses and be closer to what Christians would call *moral*?

CASPER: I don't have a single answer for that. For me, obviously, it doesn't come down to one thing, like God. There are myriad experiences, people, and forces at play. Maybe I'm just lucky. I never feel that my freedom must somehow come at the expense of others, but I'm starting to see how that may not always be the case.

For example, I mentioned how I insist on being free with my ideas and expressing myself. And I am. And that sounds really good on the surface. But one thing I've noticed is that freely speaking my mind can often and unintentionally impinge on the freedom of others. Other people may not be equipped to deal with my way with words, and my "freedom" in this case intimidates them. So in this case, my "guide" is *experience*.

I've noticed that there are consequences that sometimes result from what I see—and what I think most people would see—as a fair pursuit of personal freedom in speaking one's mind. Just because it's *fair* doesn't mean it's *friendly*. Experience is one thing I rely on. And it doesn't necessarily have to be my *own* experience.

I read a lot, and not just mysteries and sci-fi (though I do love Raymond Chandler and Philip K. Dick). In a lot of what I read, I learn. You can read *Crime and Punishment* and learn more about a guilty conscience than probably most of us would like to know. You can read *Catcher in the Rye* and learn all about the challenges and the costs of being authentic in a world that prizes style over substance. You can read the teachings of Buddha and learn that all suffering comes from putting yourself first and all happiness comes from putting others first. You can read the Gospels and learn that humility is one of the greatest gifts you can give your fellow man.

And speaking of our fellow man, that's probably where

I get most of my inspiration when I think about my pursuit of freedom. It might be from someone like Jim or a guy like Jason Evans of the Ecclesia Collective (I visited Jason's house church in *Jim & Casper Go to Church*)—both of whom set a pretty good example; they're as free as can be, people who apparently live the exact lives they want. Or it could be from people like my parents, both of whom you could safely call freethinkers.

Then there are *anti-example*s, people I've known or seen who have paid a terrible price for confusing hedonism with freedom.

What's weird is that our society seems to have replaced or confused freedom with *pursuing one's desires*. We think that being free means doing anything we want. Mainstream media and television certainly reinforce this idea. But if you're really, truly free, you're not chained down by your "wants."

So, when people try to reason with me that I should become a Christian because "Jesus will set me free," like He has supposedly set them free, they lose me. I don't need Jesus to free me from my wants or selfish desires. Even more, I think that choosing to follow Jesus for such a reason is just a continuation of serving our own selfish needs: "I used to be a drug addict; now I'm addicted to Jesus." What a drag it must be for Jesus, who said, "Serve others," to be followed around by people who only follow Him because they have replaced one addiction (or selfish need) with another.

Anyway . . . the freest people I have met aren't chained to their needs and wants, and that includes what they may or may not need or want from others. I know there is a great desire for anyone who read our first book to see me become a Christian. I know this is something Jim wants for me as well, but I also know that this "want" of Jim's is not front-and-center in our relationship. It doesn't chain him down in the slightest because I think his want is tremendously overshadowed by his interest in me and in others. And that works for me.

JIM: I love Casper's transparency. It convicts me. It makes me want to be more open, honest, and real. When he says, "The freest people I've met aren't chained down by what they want," it reminds me of one of my favorite sayings from Jesus: "For whoever wants to save their life will lose it, but whoever loses their life for me will find it" (Matthew 16:25). Since I stopped comparing my best with Casper's worst, I find myself hearing the voice of Jesus more often in our conversations together.

My religious side project, Otherlyness, gives me the framework I need to learn from Casper or anyone else who is speaking the truth in love.

CASPER SAVES A CHRISTIAN

JIM: Young Life's Washington Family Ranch is situated deep in the high desert wilderness of Central Oregon, in an area so remote it has no cell phone reception and "online mapping tools and personal GPS devices may not give you accurate directions."[23] Most notably, it is a place once known as Rajneeshpuram. It was there that Casper and I discovered one of our first converts.

The ranch property was originally developed as a commune in the early 1980s by Bhagwan Shree Rajneesh, a New Age spiritual leader who eventually fled the country after being accused of immigration violations and after several of his followers were arrested for crimes such as arson, wiretapping, and attempted murder (for poisoning the salad bars in ten restaurants in the county seat in an effort to influence a local election).

At one time, as many as seven thousand people were estimated to be living in Rajneeshpuram. When the Bhagwan drove the red roads (in the days of Rajneeshpuram, much of the campus and all of the roads were painted red) in one of his custom-made Rolls Royces, throngs of his mostly upper-middle-class, college-educated devotees strained to capture a peek of him through the luxury auto's tinted windows.

Now a whole new group of mostly upper-middle-class, college-educated folks were straining to get a peek inside the mind and heart of my atheist colleague, Casper.

A campus ministry from the University of Washington had taken over the facility for a weekend and invited us to be the guest speakers. They wanted us to "tell our story" followed by nonstop questions.

Casper and I normally tag-team at these events. I open the session with how we met and then hand it off to Casper. He tells the story of our meeting from his point of view, we read a few pages from our book, and then get into the meat of things by opening the floor for questions from the audience.

The Q&A session can go on for a very long time as people find it refreshing to ask an atheist to explain how someone can go through life with no need for God. Often we're speaking to people who have read *Jim & Casper Go to Church* and who express how they resonate with many of the same issues that affected Casper and me on our church tour.

At one point, as Casper was discussing the history of the Rajneeshees with one of the Young Lifers, he asked how many people Young Life had at the ranch on a good weekend. The answer was somewhere around five hundred. Casper said, "The Bhagwan had more than seven thousand living here with him . . . if numbers are how you judge a church's success, what does that say to you, or to me, or to anyone?"

CASPER: I wasn't trying to put them on the spot or play "gotcha." I was just curious because I found the place fascinating and had done a bunch of reading about it before we came. I think I was expecting to see more people up there, too, simply because of the picture I had of what it was like when it was Rajneeshpuram.

But I remember quickly answering my own question or just kind of blowing past it, as I saw some people looking aghast. I turned the conversation to a discussion of how maybe numbers don't really matter because the Bhagwan's numbers surely didn't make his way of living any more appealing to me.

I don't know why people get so caught up in the big numbers. Most of the people who have wanted to "save" me belong to pretty big churches. I sometimes think they're convinced that saving me is the way to go because, hey, sixteen thousand people—all stuffed into a converted basketball arena—can't be wrong! But popularity contests mean very little to me. And I've never understood why they mean so much to so many Christians.

What's really wild is that your religion's founder wasn't even remotely popular in His day and age. Only a handful of people paid attention at the time. Mass approval meant very little to Him, clearly. Which is fine by me, as there have been some pretty destructive movements that met with mass approval—and I'm not just talking about the Bhagwan.

You don't have to go back more than one hundred years in human history and you can count dozens, if not hundreds, of events, ideas, people, and so on that were both very popular and very horrifying. So the numbers . . . well, they have never meant that much to me. Just because something or someone is popular doesn't mean there's lasting value there. But maybe that's just me: the consummate outsider.

JIM: Casper was kind of kidding about being "the consummate outsider," but there was certainly more than a grain of truth in that label for him at the Young Life camp. It was Casper's first time being surrounded by so many Christian college students.

Whenever we traveled and spoke at these engagements, I often found myself as curious about what Casper was thinking as I was about the people in the audience. Whenever I'm the outsider at a party, a class, or a church, I know I'm quite self-conscious and prepared to be treated like I'm invisible. I often wonder if I'm going to connect with these people in any way at all, let alone a meaningful way, or if they'll simply reject me and my beliefs outright. I asked Casper if he had any fear of rejection.

CASPER: I think most folks believe I have something greater to fear than rejection. I'm supposed to be fearing damnation, right? Imagine what it feels like to know that just about everyone sitting there listening to you, being nice to you in the dining hall, politely asking questions in the parking lot, is also sitting comfortably—well, comfortably enough—with the image of you being tortured by Satan for all eternity.

If that's really what they believe—that the devil will be savaging me for eons—no wonder I have trouble even thinking about joining their ranks. Why would I want to be part of a group that asks me to assume that everyone who disagrees with us will be thrown into a lake of fire? That's outrageous!

It seems as if the current Christian approach to connecting with people outside the faith is either with threats or legalese. The threat is obvious—hell—and the legalese is when they start wielding the Bible's words like weapons. When Christians quote a verse from the Bible to me, I sometimes feel as if they're doing it the same way a lawyer uses case law:

"According to Corinthians, chapter X, verse Y" sounds a lot like, "According to *Brown v. Board of Education* . . ."

Part of me thinks I'm being too harsh, that what I'm saying sounds too much like an attack, because as I say it, well, it feels kind of like I'm on the attack. Y'know, you get that righteous "fire within" feeling when you're attacked. But another part of me thinks that being on the attack is a pretty reasonable response when you consider that I'm being damned or dismissed by someone I don't even know and who has never bothered to get to know me either.

The thing is, the only reason they think I'm going to burn in hell or that I'm ignorant is because I don't agree with them. They invalidate my opinion—my very life!—because I don't share their exact beliefs. It's like, no matter how I may live my life, no matter how kind or caring I may be, no matter how well I may serve others, because of that one difference, the judgment has been made, the die has been cast, and the fires are waiting for me. I'm sorry, but I just don't think there's anything remotely Christian about that—at least based on what I've read about how Jesus treated people.

And when I say this exact thing to people, their response is something like, "Oh, it's not up to me to judge; *God* will judge you. (I will simply be sitting there watching you burn, with a smug smile on my face.)" They don't actually say that last part, but it sure comes across loud and clear.

Regardless, it's not as if hearing "It's up to God" softens the blow at all. Maybe I see it this way because I don't believe in God, so as far as I am concerned, it's *you* who is consigning me to hell; it's *you* who expects to see me tortured by Satan—and that's a pretty awful thing to think about another human being.

How would you feel—how would *any* Christian feel—if I

said I was picturing you dying painfully or being tortured? Imagine it . . . it's not fun. And why would I want to be around someone—let alone *saved* and then have to be around someone for all eternity—who takes satisfaction in making someone feel that way?

JIM: Casper is quite sensitized to the hell issue because it is one of the most popular topics students like to ask about when we speak. Christians are very interested in hell, but they're also deeply divided about the size, scope, and purpose of it.

I'm currently developing a pilot project for a TV show called *Save Me*, which will bring together people from very different religious perspectives who share a common commitment to convert others. People audition by submitting a video of themselves in which they answer six questions, one of which is, *What do you believe happens after death to those who either reject or accept your beliefs?*

One guy who sent in his audition tape came across as a very kind person, a very thoughtful guy, anything but a nut job. His answer to that question was calm, direct, and stunningly certain: *the lake of fire.* I admired his moxie and appreciated his transparency, but I was astounded at how calmly he said that people will spend eternity in hell in a literal lake of fire.

The fact is, many Christians have been trained to speak very matter-of-factly about hell, with a casual kind of certainty, even though many of us lack the capacity to envision it ourselves. I think Christians are just as put off as many non-Christians by the current idea of hell; but of course we don't admit those doubts to non-Christians, lest our uncertainty exacerbate their uncertainty.

CASPER: Here's what feels so weird to me about the way Christians talk about hell. I think it was maybe the second day we were at the Young Life camp in Oregon, and I was chatting with a guy during lunch about how maybe a church or even a faith need not have mass followers to be something constructive and inviting and life-changing. Look at Jesus when He was first getting going: *twelve* disciples. By those numbers, during His lifetime He was a failure, whereas a guy like Jim Jones was a success. So again, I don't get hung up on the numbers. And I don't see myself getting saved just because "everyone else is doing it."

Anyway, it was a really nice conversation, one of the typical interactions I had with folks at mealtimes the few days we were there. The funny thing—rather, the sad, disheartening thing—was the guy I had the numbers chat with (we'll call him "Bob") was one of the people who quickly and easily raised his hand when I asked who thought I was going to hell.

JIM: Casper is referring to what we call "the hell question." It goes like this: After people have spent a couple of hours listening to Casper and me, laughing with us, learning from us, I like to break through all the *kumbaya* stuff by asking this question: "Now that you've gotten to know Casper, heard his heart, and laughed with him . . . how many of you think he's going to hell?" I ask them to raise their hands in front of Casper, who is anxious to see the response.

The room goes silent and people shoot quick glances to their right and left to see who will raise their hand. Because these are Bible-believing evangelicals, they're technically obligated to answer that question in the affirmative. They have to forget that Casper is a human being and face the brutal fact that he is going to hell. It's just that normally no one requires them to "come out" and say it to his face. In this case, here at Young-Life-formerly-Rajneeshpuram, 90 percent of the kids in the room raised their hands, saying that Casper would be spending eternity in hell.

CASPER: My jaw dropped at this. That was a pretty serious total. I thought, *Wow these kids are too young to be this judgmental*, and I remember trying to lighten things up by saying something along the lines of, "Well, that's darn rude" in my best David Letterman tone of voice, but then I saw Bob with his hand in the air, so I called him out.

I said, "We just ate a sandwich together, laughed together, and now you casually agree to picture me being tortured for all eternity in the lake of fire?" He kind of laughed, like, "Sorry man . . . you're a nice guy and all, but . . ."

If someone would say, "Hey, we want to hang out with you in heaven," that would be a wonderful thought. But it seems they usually stop at the "you're gonna burn" part. It just feels as if I will be punished for not sharing what they believe, for not being exactly like they are. Is that really how the world of God works? People are punished just for being different? Were I to believe, I think I'd find it harder to believe in an angry God who comes down on people for being "lost" than to believe in a loving God who accepts all, "lost and found." So if someone's goal is really for me to become a Christian, there are better ways to do it than by threatening me.

Most parents, for example, know that there are many ways to get their kids to *do* something, but punishment, or the threat of punishment, is so shortsighted. "Clean your room or no TV!" gets a kid to clean his room once. "Clean your room every day this week and you will start getting an allowance" works waaaaaay better. And yes, I know this from being a dad and trying various things to get my kids to see things my way.

Still, the promise of heaven, the threat of hell . . . these don't bring me closer to anything because I currently don't believe that either exists. Maybe if Christians kept that in mind when talking to non-Christians, we'd have a little more common ground. Case in point, I think, is what Jim and I do. He is not aggressively trying to bring me over to his way of thinking; he is not using language and Bible verses I don't relate to, or cajoling me or threatening me with things I don't believe in. We simply share our views, stay respectful, and that's what makes a difference.

If Jim were to start telling me that I'll burn in hell if I don't become a Christian but will go to heaven if I do, it would definitely be game over . . . and not in a good way. I mean, how much longer do you think our friendship would last if he took the "heaven or hell" path?

Same goes on my end, of course. Could you imagine how it would feel if I started telling Jim, "There's no such thing as God; you're stupid; you're gonna burn in hell—well, hell doesn't exist, but you get my meaning, pal," every time he mentions God or Jesus (which he does a lot)? How long do you think Jim would stick around? I don't understand why people think their carrot or their stick is the answer to anything.

JIM: I agree with Casper. This is why I believe he and I are far more interested in *defending the space*—that is, keeping an open and honest dialogue going between us—than in arguing about the faith. Speaking of which, here is what happened when Casper had a follow-up encounter with his friend.

CASPER: As we were about to leave, Bob flagged me down. I figured he wanted to say, "Thanks a lot for being here. We really appreciate you taking the time, etc." You know, the standard pleasantries. And he did say all that, but then he really surprised me by saying, "I wanted to tell you how sorry I was for raising my hand. I don't know if you're going to hell or what . . . and even if I did know, well, not much good comes from anyone being judgmental. You're a nice guy and you've given me a lot to think about."

I felt really, truly happy. I felt like . . . well . . . a little like I'd *saved* someone. And the best part was that it wasn't as if I made him an atheist or made him "take my side," or whatever. It was just a natural moment of personal growth for both of us. It felt like what I would think most folks would call *grace*. I'm not saying that in that moment I felt saved or anything, but it just felt like a step in the right direction. I realized that there can be *moments* that change a person.

I know there is a "moment" that can be important to many Christians: the moment they got saved. But I have been kind of suspicious of this way of thinking and have long believed that real and lasting change can only be gradual. However . . . life takes unexpected turns, and now I see that sometimes there may be opportunities for everything to change in an instant. That's kind of what this felt like.

I think his apology made me feel like what we're doing—Jim and I, writing a book, talking to people, and so on—may be more than a spiritual sideshow for the Christians we meet. In some cases, I have definitely felt like a bit of a circus freak for some folks: "Come see the fire-breathing atheist! Bring your Bible verses! Bring tomatoes!" But after that moment there, I thought, *Wow . . . maybe we can actually connect with people doing this, and maybe change a few hearts in the process.*

My heart was also changed a bit that day. I hope our paths cross again someday. That would be pretty cool because I'm not sure if he knows the impact he had on me.

JIM: I can see why this might have made that young man feel like he was "taking the high road." After all, he may have just found a way to move closer to dialogue and away from debate, or at least he learned a little about how it feels when you casually damn someone.

I hope he reads this book and discovers what a difference he made. I know it couldn't have been easy for him to "break ranks" and reach out with an apology. This is precisely why Casper and I do this—to open people's minds, create dialogue, foster mutual respect and understanding, and build relationships. It is beneficial for everyone when these things happen, whether or not you can add another notch to your salvation belt.

CASPER: It was a pretty big deal to see the impact we can have on people and to better realize the impact they have on us. There are many ways to stick in someone's mind, and though there are certainly some folks who can make a positive lasting impression like Bob did, there are others who make a lasting impression in an entirely different way.

I keep going back in my mind to that church in Kansas City where Jim and I were doing our thing—which has really never been anything more than talking to each other—and a woman called me "evil." Hearing that you're going to hell is one thing; but hearing that you may qualify to *rule* over hell is something else entirely. Part of why I wanted to hear more from that woman was because I don't think I had heard the word *evil* attributed to me before—not that I'm in any way recommending this as a conversation starter. But in my mind, I was like, *Me? Evil? Really?* And I wondered if I looked scary or like a tough guy or a demonic Fonzie or something.

She piqued my curiosity. And I think maybe, like with my friend at Young Life, I thought if I could help her become a little less afraid of me, maybe she would become a little less judgmental. I may be a lot of things, but I don't believe *evil* is one of them. But evil . . . good . . . in the end, there's only so much I can do about what people think about me.

As a matter of fact, when our talk was over, I saw her in the meeting room having coffee, and I just waited until she saw me. Then I said "hi" and kind of waved a little bit and she came over. The first thing she said was, "I'm sorry, but . . ." and I just said, "No need to be sorry." She gave me kind of a tight-lipped smile and let me know that, while her words may have been a bit stronger than she intended, she did think I was going to hell and for the rest of the congregation to sit by and act like that wasn't going to happen was shocking to her.

I said, "Well, maybe not everyone thinks that." About that time, a guy came up to us and said to the woman, "I would rather have one hundred nonbelievers like Casper in my church than one judgmental person like you." Suddenly, there I was, stepping in between them and saying something like, "Hey, can't we all just get along?"

They settled down, but I think only because they had both just heard Jim and me speak, so it kind of gave me a little influence I might not ordinarily have had. I wasn't just some guy on the street. I was, after all, the Guest Speaker. But what struck me was that this woman, while politely calling me evil, was also expressing concern for my eternal well-being. Talk about a mixed message.

I've seen this more than once—a kind of love/hate thing going on, often within the same person. Some folks perfectly encapsulate all that's possibly wrong and right with Christianity. They have both a compassionate streak and a judgmental streak. I feel for them because it can't be easy walking around with such warring forces in your heart and head. It's as if they're saying to themselves, *"How do I save all these awful, evil people?"*

I know this example is a little extreme—after all, most people don't call me *evil*; they just say that I'll basically be in the company of evil people in hell forever—yet, it strikes me as pretty standard. Almost every Christian I've met who thought I was going to hell did not seem to carefully consider how their words would affect me. It's like someone comes up to you, sticks a knife in your belly, and then wants to know how you're doing. "You're awful and evil, and I want you to spend eternity with me in heaven." *What?!?*

I always want to be careful with this because it's not every Christian I meet who is like this, but there have been so many that it really sticks with me and I just don't understand why so many Christians seem intent on starting off on the wrong foot. Is there a book or a teaching out there, or a verse in the Bible, or anything Jesus ever said that conveyed the message, "To save someone, you must first insult them"?

Right after breaking up the fight between the two Christians about my eternal destiny, I was approached by another woman from the same church, who asked, "So what should we do?"

"About what?"

"What should we do to save this church?"

I was dumbstruck: She was asking me—a person with less vested interest in that church than perhaps anyone else in the entire room—what they should do to save it. And I had what sounds like a snarky answer too. I said, "Do you believe that Jesus Christ was the Son of God and that when you die you will meet Him in heaven?"

"With all my heart," she said.

"Then you should probably sell this church and everything in it as soon as possible and give all the money to the poor, because I think that's what Jesus told people to do."

What was refreshing was that she didn't get mad at me or even react—though looking back on it, I think she certainly had a right to. She readily admitted that selling the church and everything in it was not a possibility, but we kind of smiled over the idea nonetheless. She went on to tell me that she worked there and was very concerned about the future of her church. She said attendance was dropping; they were having to let staffers go and do other kinds of belt-tightening, so I asked, "Why does this building matter so much? Does your faith depend on these bricks, that chair, this stuff?"

She said, "No," and it seemed as if no one had ever said what was to me a pretty simple truth: It's not about the building. It's not even about the church. When I look back on these events, I think there's more I could have done. Namely, I could have done a better job with the woman who called me evil. It bothers me to know that she's still out there thinking I'm evil. And I probably could have come up with a better answer for the woman who asked me how to save her church. In fact, I still have a lot of questions of my own for her.

JIM: What Casper encountered with the first woman wasn't dialogue. It wasn't even debate. It was just an attack, and as I'm sure you know, that is anything but what Jesus told us to do. Whenever I see someone open a conversation by insulting the other person, it makes me wonder: *Are we at war with ourselves and beyond redemption?*

But before we criticize her, we must realize that we've all done things like that at one time or another. We may not have started with an outright insult, but we've started from a place of judgment rather than relationship. Part of what Casper and I are trying to achieve when we speak to a group of Christians is to help people move a little bit on their "judgment meter." This capacity, while intellectually and often theologically uncomfortable, provides us a way to stay connected with people who are supposedly our ideological enemies.

I think what happened with the second woman is that she set aside her focus on the "Great Commission" and gave herself permission to see Casper as a person to connect with, rather than to "save." (After all, most Christians would never ask an atheist how to save a church.) As a result, she discovered that she *liked* him and decided to extend a tiny bit of trust. What's amazing is that this took place subconsciously and in a matter of minutes.

In her book *Being Wrong*, Kathryn Schulz comments on our tendency to judge each other. She says we place those who disagree with our beliefs into one of three categories:

1. Ignorant—lacking information;
2. Idiot—lacking a brain;
3. Evil—lacking a conscience.[24]

The woman who called Casper *evil* had him solidly pegged in category 3 of her judgment grid. But after she talked with him during the coffee hour after the event, he was inching closer to category 1. Why? His refusal to debate her and "take her on" likely surprised her. And though I wish that she could see him as something other than ignorant, well, ignorance beats evil.

With the woman who asked Casper how to save her church, we see something else entirely. Clearly, she recognized that whatever was happening inside her church was not enough to save it. So she needed to go outside. Casper gave her something she lacked—good information from an outsider.

We tend to become more open to people from whom we think we can gain something. The relational tilt came because Casper had enough discipline not to treat her the way he had just been treated by one of her fellow churchgoers. Though there could easily have been a Do Not Enter sign on Casper's door after being dubbed "evil," instead she found a welcome mat.

Many Christians have been trained to see Casper and any nonbeliever as a threat. That threat is then classified as evil, idiotic, or ignorant. With the first woman, Casper was able to move the needle from "evil" to "ignorant," but with the other woman (who may have seen Casper as ignorant at first), the results were far more interesting and helpful. She followed her intuition and discovered that, rather than lacking something, Casper may actually have something her church needed.

Trying to explain these sudden reversals in Christian logic to Casper gets complicated. I'm a Christian and I find it confusing too. The ease with which we transition between dispatching people's souls to hell and inviting them to our Christmas programs is astounding.

Without question, Christians could bring a reasonable indictment against many atheists for not giving us the benefit of the doubt and automatically assigning evil motives to us. However, there is one significant difference between our two movements: We Christians have a leader whom we claim is still alive and who told us to love our enemies and treat others the way we would like to be treated. We have a book that we take pride in memorizing and claim as God's Word. As far as I've been able to ascertain, atheists have neither. What can we learn from Casper's encounters? First, we can do better in our approach when talking with atheists about what we believe and why—that is, salvage our public image. Next, when we fight amongst ourselves, we create divisions that neither serve our common purpose nor honor our common Savior. Finally, those who stand on the outside can offer a fresh perspective and much needed insight for how to save not only the "lost" souls we encounter, but also the "found" ones the church is losing from its attendance. But only if we are willing to listen.

8

WHY I'M *CURRENTLY*
A CHRISTIAN

JIM: As mentioned earlier, *currently* is an operative word in my relationship with Casper. In the Q&As that follow our live presentations, one of the most popular topics people ask Casper to address is in what ways he is similar to or different from some of the New Atheists, such as Christopher Hitchens or Richard Dawkins.

It was during one of those times that I first heard Casper use the term *anti-theist*. I wasn't sure if he had coined it or stolen it, but I really liked how it differentiated his version of atheism from the Hitchenses and Dawkinses of the world.

This distinction also proved very helpful to many of the Christians we spoke to because most of them had not stopped to think that there are many varieties of atheist, just as there are non-practicing Christians, liberal Christians, nondenominational Christians, and nominal Christians.

By describing himself as *currently* an atheist, Casper conveys two things: 1) he's happy where he is, and 2) he's open to new possibilities.

What if Christians described themselves the same way?[25] "I'm *currently* a Christian." I realize how antithetical this thought is to contemporary evangelical thinking. But based on my observations over forty years, it would be a more accurate description of the kind of Christianity many Christians actually practice. Maybe Casper is just being more honest than we are.

CASPER: I say "currently" just because it's true. Someone once asked me if I said that to "soften the blow" or to "keep the door open" for conversion. My answer was that those might be friendly side effects, but my main purpose in saying "currently" is that I welcome the fact that as I learn new things my beliefs can change . . . everything can change at any time. As a matter of fact, the only constant thing I know is that things change, so why fight it?

But if someone were to ask me, "When did you become an atheist?" I could only say I have no idea how long I've been an atheist. Plus, I have no idea how long I will continue to be an atheist. The reason I say the former is that there was not some "Eureka!" moment, no day I celebrate or honor as the birth of my atheism. It was simply gradual, as I think most real and lasting change in one's belief system usually is.

The reason I say the latter is that I am not 100 percent certain there's not a God or gods. From what I have seen so far, gods can neither be proven nor disproven in any empirical sense—the way I have heard Jim say at some of our events that he can't say there's a God the same way you can hold up a chair and say, "This is a chair," so who knows? Maybe one day something will happen in my life that leads me to become a believer. *But*, based on what I currently have seen and believe, I am an atheist. Tomorrow? Who knows?

JIM: What Casper says actually sounds very similar to how I have seen many people become Christians. The majority of people who claim to be Christians cannot point to an epiphany moment. In fact, most people become Christians quite slowly. They take years to decide, and even then their path is often littered with a lot of "one step forward, two steps back" experiences.

CASPER: I always wondered, why is it that at so many of the churches we visited—Joel Osteen's comes to mind—the leaders demand that *moment*, that decision, the altar call? I know that moments of profound change can occur, but it seems there's an overemphasis on "The Thing" happening . . . the person rises up, walks to the altar, and—*boom!*—saved. Why does that happen? Does it last? Why does choosing Christianity have to be—for some anyway—a "Eureka!" thing?

JIM: I think the simple truth to what Casper calls the "Eureka thing" is that *it sells*. Those instantaneous transformation stories are sexy! They make us Christians feel like we're on the right side. But while dramatic conversions get most of the ink, in reality, most conversions are more journey than jump.[26] Frankly, if Christians were as transparent about their journeys as Casper is about his, many would admit that their commitment to faith is not that dissimilar to his with nonfaith.

CASPER: I probably didn't start out this open. I've probably become more transparent because I talk to Christians a lot. I write books with them and go on their radio shows.

I get asked by a few atheists I know, "Why do you do all this? Why do you work so much with Christians?" My response is always, "Well, why not?" It's a fantastic opportunity to get out there, and—I hope—put a more positive face on atheism and maybe effect a little change in the people I meet along the way. I'm just lucky, I guess, but my Christian friends would probably call it *being blessed*.

I am not entirely sure why other atheists don't take the same approach about their nonfaith. I have heard (and I don't remember where or how) that Dawkins, et al, need to be heavy-handed to make it "safe" for other atheists to "come out." They're playing to their audience—or preaching to the choir, if you prefer—and perhaps their aggressiveness gives those "atheists in hiding" the tools they need to feel confident enough to simply talk about their own beliefs. (You have to admit: There's more talk about atheism today than there was before books such as *The God Delusion* hit the market.)

But I think that when you're preaching to the choir, you're perpetrating a kind of lazy divisiveness and unnecessarily cutting yourself—and your choir—off from a whole host of other people. For me, life and living is about connecting with other people, regardless of what they do or don't believe when it comes to spiritual matters.

Unlike the apologists in either corner—atheist or Christian—I don't see how throwing down the gauntlet makes the world a better place. I think bringing people together and connecting them is a far better motivation. If what you're trying to accomplish is changing how people *think*—that is, converting them to the way *you* think—you'll never succeed if you can't even connect with them in the first place.

And if you connect with someone and don't change them, so what? You "did the work," as it were, and made the connection. I currently believe that the more people you can connect with who hold different views from yours, the more you will grow personally. So when it comes to connecting with others who have different viewpoints, Hitchens (rest his no-soul) and Dawkins are by and large ineffective.

I don't mean they're not smart. They're waaaaaaaay smarter

than I am. But for anyone to think they're going to change believers into nonbelievers by attacking what they believe, well, that's idiotic, and it accomplishes nothing other than further entrenching people.

Christopher Hitchens, in particular, seemed determined to go after believers. Just look at the title of one of his last books, *God Is Not Great: How Religion Poisons Everything*. And Dawkins, too, with *The God Delusion*. Again, not a very "can't we all get along?" title for a book. The equivalent would be a Christian book called *All Atheists Are Fooling Themselves and Will Burn in Hell*.

Dawkins and Hitchens are essentially fundamentalists. They see faith as destructive and dangerous. And though in the wrong hands faith *can* be destructive (Fred Phelps, I'm calling you out again, you easy target you!), it can be a tremendously positive thing as well.[27] The problem I have with some atheists is the same problem I have with some Christians: *certainty*. You can't unequivocally prove your beliefs, so c'mon, take it easy.

JIM: Casper is, unfortunately, not only a lightning rod for some aggressive Christians, but also for some fundamental atheists who were pretty upset with him for playing nice with Christians. When Casper was asked to submit an article to a popular atheist blog, I didn't know if atheists would welcome him with open arms or what, but man, did they ever get mean. They gave him a grade of D+, saying his arguments were weak, and so on.

CASPER: In their defense, I did offend them by insulting (playfully, in my opinion) some people they hold in high esteem. And one person on the comment board totally got it right when he or she said I was a lot more careful not to offend Christians than I was not to offend atheists.

JIM: Christians use the same "circle the wagons" approach when one of their own is attacked. I've told many audiences of Christians that, in general, we appear much more concerned about our reputation among insiders (Christians) than among outsiders (nonbelievers).

By comparison, Jesus bent over backward to ensure that His reputation with sinners was unassailable, but He was way too casual about managing His reputation with the religious folks—which is one reason they eventually killed Him. I recently read this definition of belief: "The very word *believe* comes from an Old English verb meaning 'to hold dear,' which suggests, correctly, that we have a habit of falling in love with our beliefs once we've formed them."[28]

Is it possible that in the same way many Christians have elevated *beliefs* to the point of worshipping certainty, the New Atheists (or anti-theists, as Casper calls them) have fallen in love with their own nonbeliefs?

CASPER: Without a doubt. The passion for beliefs crosses all lines, especially when there's a perceived attack. That's when defensiveness and self-righteousness eclipse our more noble motives. And there's nothing more intoxicating than self-righteousness, no matter what side you think you're on. Based on what I read and see online and on TV, I believe that self-righteous indignation has eclipsed baseball as America's favorite pastime.

When it's time to circle the wagons, our blood starts pumping, endorphins are released, and away we go; but that's just the physical side of things. As human beings—whether Christian, atheist, or anything else—we all like to think that our rational minds are in charge, not our physiology. But in this equation, the feeling we get from battling over the beliefs we have chosen supersedes any discussion: The battle itself becomes the thing. That's true of atheists and Christians alike. Many atheists have gotten more comfortable with conflict than with compromise, with self-righteousness rather than humility, with debate rather than dialogue.

Want to change people? Start by connecting with them. How? First, do no harm! Don't attack them! I know that for as long as I'm alive and long afterward, *beliefs* are here to stay. So for my money, the best approach to connecting with people who believe is probably through their own belief system. Which is what I do daily.

For example, I remember talking with a couple who put me up for the night after one of our speaking gigs. I think it was in Minneapolis. I was a little nervous at first because they seemed a little too eager to have me spend the night. I anticipated going to their home and walking into the middle of a Bible study group or some kind of atheism intervention thing. I think they might have been a little antsy too. After all, this was probably their first time inviting an "out" atheist into their home, let alone to spend the night.

So we were sitting at their kitchen table, talking. They had more questions about the book, and I answered a few, but I knew this was not what I wanted to do for the rest of the night—basically, do the "Jim and Casper Show" all over again. So I just asked them, "When did you both become Christians?" And away we went.

Immediately, the conversation became galvanizing. We talked until the wee hours, and I learned that the husband had only recently become a Christian, whereas his wife had been born again more than seven years before him. And during those seven years, they had maintained a healthy and ongoing dialogue about their continuing differences.

I asked what would have happened if the husband had never become born again, or if the wife had decided at some point to become "un-born-again." They said they had made the decision to love each other first and that was what took precedence. But they also said that my question wasn't all that relevant because they believed their love for each other was fueled by their love of God.

Toward the end of night, I pointed out how what they had done over those seven years was far more impressive than anything Jim and I had done, and I think they might have agreed. At least, I hope they did.

The point for me was that I got to know these people deeply within a few hours simply by asking them about their beliefs, by focusing on *connecting* with them rather than trying to get them to see things "my way." If I had stood there barking about "how awesome my beliefs are and how stupid yours are," it would have been an unpleasant evening for everyone. So I guess what I've found is that it makes my life more enjoyable and rewarding to ask other people about their lives.

Most religious belief systems—Christianity, Judaism, Islam, Buddhism, Hinduism, etc.—have something pretty positive at their core: Be kind to others, don't be a jerk. You can find iterations of the Golden Rule in most all of them. And I think atheists follow this Golden Rule, too. Every atheist I know, anyway. After all, you don't want to make the case against you (and/or atheism in general) an easy one by being a self-serving jerk all the time. So in that sense, we already have some wonderful common ground, no matter what the rest of our beliefs may be. I have found that talking about this common ground, this core, is effective, both in creating positive relationships and effecting a little change along the way.

Obviously, not every atheist sees things the same way I do. For some folks—again, on *all* sides of the equation—the only common ground is the battleground. And though I like to try different things at dinnertime, some folks only want red meat. But that's too easy, in my opinion.

Anyone can throw a juicy steak to their followers—look at any number of anti-theist or Christian activists—but I'm not looking for red meat. I don't need to shore up my defenses with apologetics or arguments. I'm looking for *connection*, *honesty*, and *insight*. I'm trying to see and understand—and learn from—how one's beliefs make him or her a better person and make the world a better place.

JIM: Casper's analogy about having only red meat for dinner—and the lack of variety it offers—is a good illustration of something we touched on earlier—the problem with the Christian tendency to isolate ourselves from differing opinions and commune only with other believers.

After being in close proximity with atheists over the past five years, I've observed that they typically don't like being categorized, and, for the most part, they believe that atheism is not a *belief*. But I wondered whether atheists felt a need to gather together and share their thoughts about nonbelief, explore texts that support their argument that there isn't a God, and plan events to exercise their lack of faith. Though this sounds a bit trite, it is a core human trait to long for community and to surround ourselves with like-minded people. Surely atheists are not excluded from this basic natural desire. Sure enough, when I typed "atheist support group" into Google, I got almost 2.8 million results.

CASPER: I don't speak for any other atheists; in fact, I find it strange every time someone asks me, "What do other atheists think about _____?" How would I know what other athe- ists think? I typically try to make light of the question. It's not as if I go to an atheist meeting house somewhere, where we celebrate our nonbelief and say things like, "May no god be with you . . . and also not with you." Some people without God clearly need, or at least enjoy, the sense of community that houses of God give so many.

Personally, it's not my thing. It's not that I don't like other atheists. They're usually fine by me. But with more than a few of the atheists I've met, there's not a whole lot to talk about when the subject turns to belief. They just dismiss it outright. And when I put my position forward—that I'm currently an atheist and that beliefs can change—they often dismiss me outright too. I find agnostics a little more interesting.

My dad (who is an atheist) calls me an agnostic because of my use of the word *currently*. I guess in his book—and that of many others—to say anything other than an unequivocal "no" puts one somewhere on the agnostic chart. I'm okay with folks seeing me that way, my dad included. But in my mind, I'm not an agnostic.

I see agnosticism as a way to have a "squishy" belief in God or a higher power of some kind. Agnostics, as I would describe them, believe there's "something," but they just don't know what it is. Which to me sounds like they're kind of on the fence. To be honest, that does bother me a little. In my opinion, arriving at a point of view that leaves you sit- ting on the fence seems kind of lazy. I would take Socrates' famous saying, "The unexamined life is not worth living," and tweak that a little bit to say, "The unexamined belief is not worth having."

When I meet an actual agnostic—and there are *far* more people willing to "come out" as agnostics than as atheists—I usually have a wonderful conversation. The one thing that bugs me, though, is when they use "I'm an agnostic" as a euphemism for, "I've never really looked into any of this stuff. I'm not curious about any of these questions."

It is apathy that I really find off-putting. The person who says, "I don't care whether there's a God or not or why we're here," is more rare than an atheist or an agnostic. I find people like that pretty unsettling. There's something nearly sociopathic about that level of apathy. "I don't care" is the worst thing in the world a person can say; because for my money, it's caring that makes the world work. And whether you're currently an atheist, currently a Christian, or currently whatever, as long as you at least *care*, we will have some common ground.

JIM: I like how George Hunter puts it: "In a pluralistic society, the possibility of conversion . . . is opened up through conversations with people who live with a contrasting view of reality."[29] By being "currently" whatever we are, we fully embrace where we are while leaving the door open for growth. This "open" mentality brings us directly into the moment to be actively and attentively who we are and what we believe. It serves as an opportunity to be more active in whatever faith (or nonfaith) we have.

HOW TO SAVE AN ATHEIST

JIM: While people from a wide variety of backgrounds will find something interesting in "the Jim and Casper story," it's evangelical Christians, people who care deeply about convincing others to "accept Christ as their personal Savior," who are probably our most curious audience. Both Casper and I have the utmost respect for people who are serious about their convictions. And while the two of us may disagree about what informs and shapes those convictions, we respect those who respectfully hold them. We also realize that although our project is very, very niche (who else do you know doing what we do?), it nonetheless has far-reaching ramifications.

Our country is getting more diverse, not less. Interest in religion is not going away anytime soon, and atheism is here to stay as a viable option for Americans. As one thinker so aptly put it, "The future belongs to those who take the present for granted."[30] I shared that quote with Casper, and it got him thinking.

CASPER: Interesting quote. What I think "take the present for granted" means in our context is that the future belongs to those who can accept and embrace things as they are, not those who agonize over how things (in the present) should be. We can't accept the present without learning to live with people who hold views and beliefs dramatically different from our own. As odd as it may sound coming from an atheist, I believe those who take this "for granted" will be more effective evangelists than those who don't.

JIM: In an attempt to help you adjust to this "new normal," and in keeping with our modus operandi, Casper and I agreed it might help to close with some direct Q&A. I will present some pointed questions that I believe might be on your mind (because these questions—in one form or another—have been asked of me hundreds of times by Christian audiences ever since *Jim & Casper Go to Church* hit the shelves), and Casper will respond.

Here is our disclaimer: We're both mindful that we've been given a unique platform, and we're aware we do not represent the majority views of either Christians or atheists.

Let's say you once said, "I'll never be that kind of person or I'll never change my beliefs" and then you did. Casper, have you ever changed your beliefs about something significant?

CASPER: My atheist dad gave the eulogy at my Catholic mother's funeral. He said toward the beginning, "I can best sum up my beliefs as follows: none." It was a powerful statement and it made me proud and confused all at the same time.

Is that what it means to be an atheist? Beliefs = none? I think many Christians would agree. After all, a Christian synonym for atheist is "nonbeliever." So if I can't have beliefs that stay steady or change, can I instead have hopes realized or dashed, values held or abandoned, purposes achieved or incomplete? What's the difference? I don't see too much.

The simple answer to this question, then, is yes. I have many times believed things would be or go a certain way, and then they didn't, which meant I then believed something else. Or I believed things ought to be a certain way and eventually saw they weren't, and so again, my beliefs changed.

For example, go back in time . . . meet me in my mid-twenties and ask me, "Hey, Casper, do you believe you'll one day write a book for a Christian audience about how to save your atheist soul?" I would have said, "I don't believe so." And yet . . . here we are.

JIM: Christians want to know if there is anything that periodically moves you toward being more open to the idea of God. Since we can't physically get inside your head and pull whatever levers we need to pull to change your beliefs, what *is* up for grabs?

CASPER: I wish it were as simple as telling people, "A hot cup of black coffee with two shots of espresso and a fresh, hot, glazed donut a couple of times a week," because then I would be more likely to enjoy a hot cup of black coffee with two shots of espresso and a fresh, hot, glazed donut a couple of times a week.

In truth, it may be even more simple than that. Just self-lessly live the values Jesus spoke about, such as *compassion*. When I see someone demonstrate real, selfless compassion, it affects me. And when acts of compassion are undertaken by people who believe in a loving God . . . well, what can I say? The walk is being walked.

And don't be confused about compassion: Compassion is putting the needs of others in front of your own—especially the needs of people who can't help themselves: the poor, the homeless, the sick, you know who I'm talking about. This can be as basic as giving a sandwich to a street person or opening a free health care clinic in a poor neighborhood or simply withholding judgment when a friend comes to you in times of trouble. Sometimes compassion is as easy as being quiet.

Sometimes the things a Christian can do to move a non-Christian closer to being more open to the idea of God are even simpler: Every time Jim and I talk, or every time my friend Jason Evans has me over to his house, for example. I know that both guys are 100 percent believers; that's the foundation of their lives. But, to continue the foundation analogy, when I am invited into someone's home, we don't walk into the basement and look at the foundation. We usually sit in the living room or on the porch. The foundation is always there, but it's not always the center of our attention.

In the end, I think the best way to keep me "open" is when people remain open with me. Tell me who you are. I will tell you who I am and we can accept each other as we are. Telling me I'm wrong for being who I am . . . that won't bring me closer to you, and it certainly won't bring me closer to your God.

Some people think the way to bring me closer to God is to prove me wrong in how I live my life. They want me to be open to finding God, and yet the first thing they do is throw up a roadblock by trying to show me I'm wrong. That's wrong. And we know what two wrongs don't make!

JIM: One thing you have in common with evangelicals is a belief in the power of marketing. We invest a lot of time and money trying to reach out to people like you. How do you like to be "sold"?

CASPER: I think that's a good point: it *is* a sell for many people. And the way I see it, that "sell" is too often tied to the "magic moment." In sales, there really is a magic moment: the decision to act, to reach for the wallet, to sign on the line which is dotted. For many Christians, there's an equivalent: the day they were saved, the moment they made the decision to act, whether that act was to walk forward to the stage and be blessed or go quietly to their knees in their own homes. They can usually recall specifically the moment they "signed on the dotted line."

But I don't think changing one's beliefs would require a sales pitch. After all, it's not like a transaction . . . or is it? "I will accept your beliefs for thirty days. If during this time I find I am happy with these beliefs, I may keep them and pay nothing for a proposed eternity in heaven. If I choose to return them, I understand that I risk damnation, for which the manufacturer of said beliefs may not be held liable."

What if it were like that? I spoke not long ago with a well-known Christian thought leader and learned that a "thirty-day trial" he and his wife undertook—of their own volition—was indeed part of what made them into Christians. They decided for thirty days to live their lives as biblically as possible and trust in God completely, turning to God for each decision. And for them, what started as a thirty-day trial became an everlasting commitment. I don't know if there's anything wrong about asking someone to "try before you buy." It's certainly an easier proposal to accept than "convert now and forever."

Imagine if that were how Christians attempted to reach non-Christians: "I don't need for you to become a Christian . . . but maybe you could just try it and see if you like it?" The first thing you could offer might be an easy first step, not a lifetime commitment. Of course, you have to be prepared for "no thanks," but that's the nature of extending any offer: a product, service, help, whatever. People might say "no thanks." So accept that. And would anyone really reply to a "no thanks" with a "see you in hell"? I would hope not.

Regardless, and on a more practical level, if you want to reach out to "people like me," I have learned from my years in marketing it's easier to convert someone from a prospect to a customer through a *pull* rather than a *push*.

When you "push market" to people, you send unsolicited e-mails, you telemarket, you place ads where and when you think your prospects might be driving, walking, whatever. Basically, you get in their faces with the kinds of questions that have only one answer: "*Yes*, I will buy." There's a time and place for push marketing, of course, and it's done because it works . . . but it doesn't last. When the push becomes evident, eventually someone gets pushed away. After all, a push goes in only one direction.

A pull goes the *other* way, a pull goes toward. When you "pull market," you do things that will naturally and eventually *attract* someone to you. You engage them, of course, but you're not saying, "So how much would you pay? But wait, there's more! . . ." With a "pull," you find ways to get your prospects to ask the questions.

I would bet there's no question a Christian would rather hear from a non-Christian than something like this: "I want to know more about your beliefs: Tell me what it means to be a Christian." If you were doing things that naturally pull outsiders toward you—such as serving them—then such questions would be a natural result. People would witness your selflessness, your servitude (it just occurred to me that serve + attitude = servitude!), and would eventually want to know what fuels it. Enter a natural dialogue on Christianity.

JIM: You've had the unusual experience of being a celebrity non-Christian in a Christian world. You get to walk into churches, get up on stage, and tell people what you think they need to know about people like you. What have you learned about Christians through this experience?

CASPER: It's probably best to say what I've learned *so far*. . . . Once I've met every Christian there is and can remember every word we exchanged and every idea we shared, then I can tell you what I've learned about Christians.

The people we've met in our travels have varied wildly. Probably because the churches we have visited vary wildly, in size, scope, geography, demography, and how they view Christianity. But one thing never failed: *hospitality*. In spite of the sometimes staginess of some of the greeters at the door, not one church we visited had a separate door for atheists. No one followed me around with a sponge and Pine-Sol, disinfecting everything I touched, whispering to others behind my back, "You don't want to sit there. An atheist was sitting there. That chair still belongs to Satan. Let me wipe it down."

I like to share this thought on hospitality because I think it's a concept or attitude that already exists within most churches, and thus it would be easy enough to build on. Imagine if churches, instead of putting something scary or insulting on their marquees (for example, "Stop, Drop, and Roll Doesn't Work in Hell" or, "Don't Be So Open-Minded Your Brains Fall Out"), or some silly pun (such as . . . almost every church marquee I've ever seen), what if that space were used to extend a real, specific expression of hospitality to the outside world? Something beyond "All Are Welcome"; something that really lets passersby know you want *them*: "This Sunday, Free Coffee for Atheists, Free Scones for Agnostics,

Free Donuts for All." Can you imagine? Try it: Before you spend another $1000 on door hangers, try spending $100 on donuts and scones and rewrite your signage. See what happens.

At the moment—writing this, thinking about this question— it appears I think I'm still on stage, telling "people like you" what I think they need to know about "people like me." I can only speak for one person like me—me—when I say I have learned that Christians are a mixed bunch. Evangelical, Methodist, Catholic, Protestant, Baptist, Anabaptist, South- ern Baptist, Seventh-day Adventist, Presbyterian, Lutheran, Episcopalian . . .

Atheists, as far as I can tell, only have the one denomination— *athe*ism—though some folks confuse *anti-theism* with atheism (and I don't blame them). Most prominent atheists continue to waste their breath attacking something they don't believe in . . . isn't that weird? "I don't believe X exists, therefore I will attack X, which doesn't exist and therefore cannot be attacked. Anyway . . . *attack!*"

Forgive the slight tangent; but it's hard to say what I have learned about Christians because I can't define in a single phrase the hundreds of people I've met. Over the past few years, I've met many wonderful people who call themselves Christians, and their kindness sticks with me and has helped me grow. Even the handful who were unkind and occasionally jerky helped me grow, too, as they gave me the opportunity to practice patience—which, as you know, is a virtue.

JIM: People accuse us of keeping you "unsaved" so we can keep our show going. What do you say to them?

CASPER: How cynical! How would that even work? Are there Bible verses you won't share with me until the "Jim and

Casper Thing" has run its course? Are there shady advisers telling you, "Don't tell Casper yet about heaven's all-you-can-eat Korean BBQ. . . . We need him unsaved until we get the audio book done. Then God can have him." Come on! Don't make me laugh.

JIM: It has been said that the way to get your kids to do what you really want them to do as adults is raise them to do just the opposite when they're kids. What if your kids show an interest in church or Jesus when they're young? How will you respond?

CASPER: Yes, that's some logic, isn't it? I've heard it before too. By that logic, I should be a psycho killer, as I definitely don't want my kids to grow up to be psycho killers.

I've also heard this question in a different form, and it always gets my dander up a little bit. Maybe it's just that, as a dad, when someone mentions my kids, my protective and defensive side (naturally and appropriately) comes out.

The first time I recall hearing this kind of question—What if your kids became Christians?—was when Jason Evans and I were invited to speak together at the Organic Church Movements Conference in 2008. It was going fairly well. There seemed to be an appreciation for the "unique friend-ship" between Jason and me, some questions about how we maintained it, how we challenged each other, and so on. Eventually, a guy got up and said, "You say you don't believe in supernatural things of any kind, but what would you do if your own daughter had a supernatural experience? What would you do if she said she saw and heard Jesus in the flesh? What would you do then?"

I felt a little like he was baiting me . . . because he was. Why would anyone ask a question like that? What was the response he thought he would get? Would I, as an atheist, somehow put my daughter "in her place" and deny her professed supernatural experience, or would my feelings for her override my atheism and would I start to see the light?

There was a clear assumption that there would be some sort of challenge or disconnect between my daughter and me if her beliefs were different from mine, and that's ridiculous and insulting. I mean, come on! Her beliefs and interests are almost 100 percent different from mine right now—she's eleven and believes in all kinds of things—and that in no way affects our connection.

Should my kids become people of faith, nothing should change between us. I'm not saying nothing will—how could I possibly know? But based on how I am raising them, I believe nothing should. When my mom converted to Catholicism, it wasn't like I cut her off, or vice versa. For us, it was one more thing to talk about, to connect on. She was worried about me, of course. After all, she was now on a path to heaven, and I was, according to her and every other Christian, lost.

Maybe that was the guy's concern, that my daughter and I would be forever separated. I wish I could say that's what it felt like, but it felt more like, "Gotcha, ya stupid atheist!" Maybe I was just feeling defensive. One thing is certain: The last thing I felt like doing was talking more to that guy. His words seemed engineered to make me feel everything from damned to a bad dad to whatever. Gotcha, indeed.

JIM: Suppose you encountered Christians who made you think they really aren't in it to change your nonbeliefs, but just to be friends. Would that work? What could a church do to "sneak up on you" spiritually?

CASPER: Why would a church want to sneak up on me spiritually? Hoping to catch me when my soul is napping and then—boom? You only sneak up on someone when you're trying to hide something, right?

We talked about this before. I think the mistake a lot of churches make is expecting the mountainous mass of people out there to *come into* the church. In my opinion, the church needs to *go out* to the people honestly and sincerely, saying, "What can we do for you?" What's so hard about that? It gives the churches what they want too: an audience with the unchurched and anyone outside their own church walls. This really is the classic win-win.

And yet, I've mostly seen churches that expect you to come to them—and preferably in desperation or with your head hung in shame. ("I'm a sinner! I'm a helpless, worthless sinner! Save me!!!") And with your wallet out. ("I'm a helpless, worthless sinner who can hand over 10 percent of my earnings! Save me!") There are many churches—too many—that have shown they'll do whatever it takes to lure you in. (Yes, I said *lure*.) Rock-and-roll music, movies, special guest stars.

What's the big hurdle here? Why can't these churches understand that the point is to serve others? Just go out there and do the work. Even if you're trying "just to be friends" in the hope that you will someday save me, do the work to be my friend.

If I recall correctly, Jesus *commanded* you to serve others. He didn't sheepishly drag His toe in the sand, look down at the ground, and say to His followers, "Well . . . I guess it would be nice if maybe you could, y'know, serve other people. If it's not too much trouble? If it works for you?" He said, "*Do this.*"

When you do the work—when you do what Jesus commanded you to do—you not only do what He expects of you, but you get a chance to meet people (the kinds of people you want in your church), *and* you set yourself up for success because the people you meet will see that you're a "walking walker," not a "talking talker."

JIM: Tell us about some Christians who have impressed you. What did they say motivated them to follow Jesus and dedicate their lives to Him?

CASPER: This question is impossible to answer, and it's not because I haven't met many Christians (and heard of or read about many more) who have impressed me. It's because the Christians who have impressed me never bothered to tell me what motivated them to follow Jesus and dedicate their lives to Him.

Jesus spoke, and these folks listened, apparently. And they didn't hear Jesus say, "I want you to go forth and tell people why you think I'm awesome." They heard Him say, "Practice justice, mercy, and faith," and that's what they do. But when I turn on the TV and there's Joel Osteen or some other televangelist telling me how his God is an awesome God (sometimes, "an awesome, AWESOME God"), I think "So what? I should sign up for what you're offering because you think it's awesome?" If I signed up for everything that somebody thought was awesome, I would have joined Club Penguin (which my kids think is awesome) a long time ago. I would be more likely to come on board if you showed me something *you* did that was awesome. And not only that, but something so awesome that I said it was awesome, not you yourself. There's nothing "awesome" about grandstanding.

Though I've met many Christians who were very impressive people, they were impressive in very different ways: this one runs a shelter for homeless people, that one helps protect the rights of migrant workers (but both clearly in line with "whatever you do to the least of my brethren").

What these impressive people have in common, and what I can only guess motivates them, is that they seem to have been able to strip Jesus of the church's—the religion's—baggage. They seem to know that, while the Bible may be two thousand years old and some of its language and cultural references may be a bit outdated, there is a core principle voiced clearly and repeatedly by the founder of their belief system: love others, be charitable, don't be a hypocrite. No matter what circumstances we may find ourselves in today, that's a timeless message.

Another "unifying force" among the Christians who have impressed me is that they are some of the least judgmental people I've met. Yes, the Bible says "judge not," but it feels as if these folks didn't need to read it or be told it to live it.

JIM: You are someone who currently claims affiliation with atheists. What is it about that group that concerns you the most?

CASPER: I don't claim affiliation, really. I requested a membership kit, but they wouldn't accept a cash payment because of the "in God we trust" thing. . . . But seriously, most of my friends are believers of one stripe or another (Christians and Jews mostly, with the occasional Muslim, Hindu, or Buddhist), and I don't really know a whole lot of atheists. The ones I do know . . . well, we don't talk much about "our group" because the point is there is no group. If we do talk about atheism, it's limited to things like, "When did you realize you felt this way? What led to your losing faith, if you had it in the first place?"

Speaking for my own atheism, it's not something I celebrate, really. Nor is it something I mourn. It's just something that *is*, for me. So while some atheists may position it as a "belief system," I don't. Comparing atheism to Christianity or Judaism or Buddhism or any belief system is like comparing apples and guitar strings. I know the typical thing to say is "oranges," but apples and oranges are both fruits with a fair amount in common. When it comes to belief and nonbelief, you're not comparing one fruit to another.

Based on what I've read, seen, and heard, I have a hard time figuring out what atheists stand for. It's very, very clear what they stand against, however. Religion. And it's a drag. And it's nothing that anyone who knows an atheist, or who has heard an atheist speak, or who has read about something an atheist said doesn't already know: Atheists don't like religion, especially organized religion (weird . . . no one complains too much about unorganized religion). We get it.

I think the thing most Christians may like to know is that many atheists, when you get down to the nitty-gritty with them, one-on-one, are not "faith haters." I feel comfortable in making an assumption that most atheists detest religion, but equally comfortable in saying that there are many atheists like me who don't detest faith in and of itself. (On a side note: While many atheists seem to detest religion, I've seen that some people with faith seem to detest atheists. If one must detest, I would prefer they detest the nonbelief, not the nonbeliever.)

We all know that faith can guide people to great things, and I have often said that if every Christian did exactly as Jesus commanded, the world would be a wonderful place. That's not to say the world would be a mess if it were devoid of faith in God. Who knows? It would definitely be a good thing if people stopped killing each other because they thought God was on their side. (Note: There's a wonderful *South Park* episode devoted to a future in which religion is obsolete and atheists are killing other atheists over which kind of atheism is superior.)

It has never been exclusively the job of people of faith to make the world a better place. We can all pitch in, and there are benevolent atheists out there too. Unfortunately, I cannot name names, as most atheists are still "closeted." For whatever reason, *atheism* is still a dirty word in America. Did you know that atheists are supposedly the least trusted group in America? I think it would probably be harder to be elected president as an atheist than with any other affiliation.

My main concern with "today's atheism" boils down to too much focus on what's destructive in religion and not enough focus on what's constructive in atheism. An oft-quoted saying from Jim, "I'll stop comparing my best with your worst," applies here. For some atheists (you know, the ones getting the headlines, flinging the red meat), it's more like, "I'll keep comparing your worst with my . . . nothing. Forget comparing anything; you're just the worst."

JIM: Many Christians say they reject atheism because without God, you can't possibly have any real sense of morality, of right and wrong. I know you probably don't agree with this, but what do you say to the question, regardless?

CASPER: This is one of my favorite myths about atheism: *When you have no God, you have no moral compass.* Well, if I may say, I feel right in saying that's wrong. However, when I'm asked for my take on morality, immorality, and right and wrong, I've told more than a few people that I don't feel as if these terms really *belong* to me; they seem too dependent on some sort of external, objective judgment, such as that which would come from God.

When it comes to beliefs and faiths, I've found that one person's "right" is almost always someone else's "wrong." Look to the Middle East and the Israeli/Palestinian conflict for immediate proof of that. I've done my best, at least since meeting Jim and working on all of this, to view ideas, opinions, and just about every human behavior and interaction as either *constructive* or *destructive*.

For me *constructive* and *destructive* are terms that are easier to objectively quantify: Does what you do or say hurt or help others? Do those "others," in turn, hurt or help? Granted, this could just be semantics. (I know it's way too easy, with any communication one finds challenging, to dismiss it as a disagreement over "semantics," but it might actually be true here.)

Anytime we have a conversation with someone with a different belief system, we're rarely—if ever—going to start with the same definition of right and wrong, the same semantics. So part of having a real conversation and connection with someone with differing views, I think, means knowing that your differences are, as often as not, merely semantic.

I have found the words *constructive* and *destructive* more conducive for building "semantic bridges" between people with very different ways of thinking. That way I'm not saying the other person is right or wrong or holy or evil or saved or damned. Instead, I'm asking if he or she is helpful or hurtful, which are definitely softer words that steer the conversation away from judging each other toward a more careful consideration of the impact of our words.

Here's another myth about atheism I'd like to quash: *If you don't put your faith in God* (that is, if you're an atheist), *then you make yourself into your own god.* This always baffled me because from an early age, I was told to believe in myself. So if I'm my own god and I don't believe God exists, then I can't believe in myself because I don't exist and . . . and . . . and then I sit there, confused.

I am not my own god, and not just because I don't have the time to worship myself—I would make time for that, buy a few more mirrors, all that. It's because the first time I heard someone say, "You're your own god," I asked what he meant by that, and he said, "You value yourself above God, above everything, really."

If that's the definition of being your own god, then I am in no way even close. It doesn't take me long to find something I value in this world more than myself. I'm a parent, after all. But my kids are most certainly not my god. My kids are the center of my world, and I recognize that making their lives better means making other people's lives better because a rising tide lifts all boats—and a better world for all means a better world for my kids. But that still doesn't seem like enough of an answer. If I have no god, what *do* I place before myself and mine?

At this stage in my life, the best answer this "currently an atheist" can provide to anyone who asks is that *you* are my god. I may not worship you or pray to you, but the mere fact of your existence (and mine) gives me something close to spiritual inspiration. This life, this living, this being here together . . . that for me is something before which I stand humbly.

Casper's Conclusion

If you're a Christian reading this book, I have a request: Please try to understand a few things from my point of view (a view that may be shared by people close to you that you would like to bring closer to Jesus). I do not believe I am unsaved. I do not believe I am lost. I do not believe I am a sinner. Those may be your beliefs (they're most certainly your words), but currently they're not mine.

So what are you going to do now?

Not about me, but about the people in your life you believe are unsaved/lost/sinners/damned-for-all-time when they say something similar to you: "Hey, you may think I'm lost, but I sure don't."

Are you really going to throw in the towel and say—literally or figuratively—"Well, to hell with you!"? What do you think will happen next if you do that? Will the people you think are lost be any more found?

Likely, the only thing that will happen is that you will

increase the distance between yourself and the people you care about. And if you're truly concerned about bringing your lost friends and family closer to God, adding distance to those relationships will do nothing to help you in your mission.

So what can you do to keep those people close to you? Try *caring* instead of *scaring*, for starters. We've talked a lot about hell in this book, and that's because so many Christians seem to think that hell is where conversations about salvation should begin. I get that. Sort of. After all, you believe that salvation is what keeps one from ending up in hell, and I understand how endlessly important that is to you.

But for most of us who don't share your beliefs . . . we don't think too much about eternal salvation—or about your version of eternity. (My vision of eternity is pretty boring, as I said: I think the same thing that happened to me before I was born will happen to me after I die, which is to say, not much.) So do you really think that's where a conversation with your favorite atheist should start? Put simply, why start with The End?

Putting me in your "unsaved" category makes me feel like it's all over. You're telling me I'm doomed—not just lost, but a lost cause; it *always* feels like a put-down. I know that's not the intent, but at best it feels as if you're telling me, "The End is near! Repent!" As far as I can see, in this day and age, that's probably not the best place to start.

So where do we start?

Maybe start by trying to see me how I see myself. I don't see myself as unsaved or wrong or doomed. I just don't currently believe what you believe, that's all. But even though I may not share your beliefs, I respect them. I've always respected Christians' beliefs, but my respect is definitely stronger now because over the past few years, I have worked so hard to understand your beliefs. Maybe that makes me different from your "garden variety atheist," but not by much (based on the atheists I know, anyway).

So I guess turnabout is fair play: Can you respect what I believe or don't believe? That would be a much better starting point than "I'm right; you're wrong." Even if you believe with all your heart that I'm wrong, try not treating me that way. Respecting our differences will always be a much better starting point for us. I know they are big differences, but starting from "we're different" beats "you're doomed" every time.

I understand it's hard to accept these (apparently) fundamental differences, so try this: Imagine that instead of talking about God, we're talking about something else—a specific type of food we enjoy—let's say, pizza. One day, you meet someone who has never tasted pizza. And it's not because they're not aware of pizza—it's all around them: there's Methodist pizza, Jewish pizza, Buddhist pizza, Lutheran pizza, Baptist pizza, non-Dominos-ational pizza.

What do you do?

Do you feel superior to this non-pizza-eating person? Probably not. You're probably just curious as to why they've never had pizza, so you ask questions. Then you might ask if they'd like to try a slice sometime. If they say no, you may say to yourself, "Okay, maybe some other time." But you don't damn them to hell, do you?

● ● ●

When I learned that Jim and I would be writing another book together, a mix of feelings overtook me: I was honored, grateful, bewildered, hopeful, anxious, elated, and more. We had talked about it, of course. We knew there might be some interest in our continuing story, and we knew the next step we would take together—what we would share with people next, what people might want to know next. We knew because people had been telling Jim (and me, a little) the one thing they wanted to know above all else: *Was I saved yet?*

After all, I had gone to church and gone to church again, and again and again and again and again and again and again and again and again . . . And if going to fifteen or twenty churches won't save someone . . . what possibly could?

Also, I was friends with many Christians. I had even spent time with some really well-known ones! Some heavy hitters! Ones who had personally saved hundreds of people! And I had demonstrated what some would call rather Christian behavior (as I hope some of this book has shown). I had been humble and charitable along the way. I had helped people. I had shown that I could turn the other cheek. I did unto others as I would have them do unto me.

So the only thing left to seal the deal, to make it official, to really help put people's minds at ease was knowing that, yes, I had accepted Jesus Christ as my personal Savior. I had stepped to the stage, gone to the altar. I had said what was expected of me, and I was now infused with the Holy Spirit and ready to spread the Good News and . . . but I didn't. And I haven't yet. And I might not. But then . . . ? Who knows?

When Jim initially suggested we call the book *Saving Casper,* I agreed. Mainly because I thought it would resonate with people, and it was also quite humbling to think I was on people's minds in what I hope would be a kind and caring manner. There's nothing wrong, in my opinion, with people hoping I get the chance to enjoy eternal life (one far away from the lake of fire, anyway).

But though Jim and I like the title, we agree that the book

is more about saving what's *between* two people than with saving just one person.

Even though the opportunity and platform Jim and I have is unique, the type of relationship we have—he's a Christian! I'm an atheist! We can still hang!—is more common than you might think. In fact, if you're reading this, you probably have friends and family members who have different beliefs from your own. I know this from talking to a lot of folks who are terribly worried about the eternal fate of their "atheist daughter" or "unchurched brother."

I don't know if being worried is the right path, though. Because in most cases, the people you're worrying about don't share your concerns, so there's no context for them there. Worrying about someone doesn't necessarily connect you with them. In fact, your worries about their "eternal salvation" are more likely to push the people you care about farther away from you. On top of that, didn't Jesus say something about not worrying about anything?

But there's light at the end of the tunnel, I think. Christians who worry about their "atheist daughter" or "unchurched brother" clearly care about these people. So why not start there? Simply care about people—and let them know you care in terms they can relate to. Letting them know you care about how they're doing *today*, rather than telling them your concerns about where they'll spend eternity, is far more appreciated and endlessly more effective if you're hoping to someday see that person "saved."

It's not that I think there is never a good time to talk about eternal salvation, but it may be one of the worst starting points you could choose if you're hoping to connect with someone who doesn't share your beliefs. Again, why start at the end? Don't start with their death. Start with their life;

start with the person; start with the here and now; start by focusing on friendship over witnessing.

I'm not saying there's no good time to share your faith. But as a starting point or as the foundation? Well, it can be tough to build a relationship between two people on a foundation that only one of them can relate to.

Jim and I "work" as we build a friendship. Our conversations about faith and beliefs are built on that bedrock. And I hope we've shown it's possible for people with different beliefs to be friends. I think it's an easier step to try to be friends with someone than to try to convert them, anyway. While attempting to be friends could possibly keep the door open for someone's conversion, attempting to convert that person may close the door to friendship.

One more thing to remember at all times: Your "atheist daughter" or "unchurched brother" is currently far more interested in your friendship than your faith. So maybe start there—with a shared interest in friendship, rather than with any effort to convert someone. (You do want to be friends with your "atheist daughter" or "unchurched brother," don't you?)

Conversion. Whose job is it, anyway? Is it Jim's job? Is it your job? Is there something wrong with Jim because he can't—or won't—convert me? (If you say yes, then let's hope you and I don't meet and become friends. Because if that happens and you don't convert me . . . then there's something wrong with you, too.)

What about God? Is saving me God's job? If God is omnipotent, omniscient, and omnipresent, then He certainly can convert me anytime He wants to, right? Sure, I have free will, but if God really wanted us all to convert right now, couldn't He just make it happen? Or is that what makes this world and all its people so interesting to Him, that we're not all going to make it to heaven? Or is this just an endless test and the loving God I've been told about is real and true, and He will, in spite of my not being "saved" in any church-recognized capacity, still be loving and forgiving and grant me eternal life anyway?

Hey, I hope that's the case, because it means I must be saved. After all:

> Not everyone who says to me, "Lord, Lord," will enter the kingdom of heaven, but only the one who does the will of my Father who is in heaven. Many will say to me on that day, "Lord, Lord, did we not prophesy in your name and in your name drive out demons and in your name perform many miracles?" Then I will tell them plainly, "I never knew you."
>
> MATTHEW 7:21-23

I have done (or at least I work really, really hard at doing) "the will" mentioned above. I do unto others as I would have them do unto me. I have served the poor and needy. (It's not like I work at a homeless shelter or anything, but I do show people kindness, a cup of coffee, and more.) I respect others. I am forgiving. Really, the only thing I haven't done, that separates me from the Christians in my life, is stand up and say, "Yes, I believe."

But wait . . . then I must *not* be saved, because, after all:

> Whoever acknowledges me before others, I will also acknowledge before my Father in heaven. But whoever disowns me before others, I will disown before my Father in heaven.
>
> MATTHEW 10:32-33

So . . . is "doing the will" enough? Is saying the words enough? Apparently not. You have to do the will, say the words, take the steps and (sometimes) wear the garment, grow the beard, take the bread and wine, don't take the wine, don't eat the meat with the cheese, face the east, wear the cross, don't wear tattoos, worship on Sunday, worship on Saturday, worship on Sunday and Wednesday, give 10 percent of your salary to the church, give one-third of your finest fruits to the Lord, give everything to the poor . . .

Is it any wonder I don't know 100 percent what it means to be saved? Most of what I've heard is about avoiding hell and going to heaven, so "getting saved" appears to be about where you end up more than anything else. And based on what I've experienced, not only is it a little hard to figure out what it takes to get there, it's also a bit blurry what's expected of someone once they're saved and before they get to heaven.

Jim and I talked at length about this in *Jim & Casper Go to Church*, and from what I could tell from Christian churches, the main thing expected of most of the saved people I met along the way was that they attend church once a week. I also learned that the main way to get saved was to stand up at the end of a service, march forward, and let the preacher lay his hands on you—et voilà!

But is this how it has to happen? Can you be saved secretly? Having lived your life as an "out" atheist—one who went public saying there is no God—can you, on your deathbed, accept God silently in your waning moments (maybe that's your only option as your motor functions aren't working properly and you can't speak) and make it into heaven? Would it matter to, or comfort, your Christian friends and family who sob by your bedside, who weren't able to hear you and who therefore think you're on your way to hell? Would they see you in heaven after they die and say, "What are *you* doing here?"

I don't speak specifically for anyone else, but I don't think it's just me who finds the whole concept of "being saved" and its rewards and responsibilities a little confusing. Being saved has to be about more than avoiding hell. It has to be about more than going to church once a week, more than saying the Lord's Prayer.

And it has to be about more than changes in your own life too, right? Because I also met some "on fire" people, recent converts who, for example, quit doing drugs after finding God. But then, in at least one case I can think of—and probably many more that you know of—they start doing drugs again. So now they still have God, but they also have drugs again. Are they still saved? Do they have to re-quit drugs and get re-saved? How many shots does a person get at this? I would say endless shots, if God is loving and forgiving. And if it is endless, then why would it end with death? Meaning, why am I required to acknowledge here on earth "before others" that I am saved? I thought it was a personal choice.

And are you really saved if the main thing you're being saved from is bad choices and bad luck? Does that mean the reckless and destitute are the only so-called "sheaves" to be brought in and the rest of us, the nonreckless, nondestitute, nonbelievers . . . well, just forget about us then? I have actually heard this case made a few times during my travels when I got into one-on-one talks with some people.

"Casper, you're an atheist. You're not our target."

What?!?

So somehow, my willingness to be open and say, "I don't currently believe there's a God," means I'm out of the running entirely? Is there biblical support for giving up on me? Are Christians really only focused on saving people "on the fence"? I can't imagine this is true.

That's why I believe the focus on whether or not I'm saved is the wrong focus; that evangelism based on outcomes (total number of souls saved) rather than processes (practicing grace to build working relationships with most everyone you meet) is always bound to fail. If you don't get the outcome you want, well, "See you later. You're not my target anyway." Throw in the towel.

The Christians I feel closest to are the ones who seem least interested in whether or not I myself am a Christian. These are people who talk very little about being saved, but who also openly discuss their faith and their doubts and would consult the Bible to inspire themselves, not to disprove me.

This feels, in my mind, closer to what it may mean to be a Christian; but guess what? I only found out about this as these particular people made a choice to befriend me rather than convert me. They kept me close, and I learned how they live their faith simply by being in their lives.

And that's what I think works. Don't show the unsaved/lost/damned people where they have gone wrong and what they should be doing and what Bible verse they may have missed. Instead, develop your friendship and simply show them how you live your faith. And though I don't think any-one on earth can objectively say, "Here's how it's done," I also know that each person can subjectively say, "Here's what living the faith means to me, and here's how I do it." And that's a perfectly good answer. Especially when shared among friends.

The clearest path to saving someone doesn't always re-veal itself immediately. You need to make sure you're there when it does (and accept that the *when* could even be an *if*). If you throw down the gauntlet—"Have you thought about where you'll spend eternity?"—you will likely force your "atheist daughter" or "unchurched brother" to turn away from you, when what I think you want is for them to turn toward you. And that means keeping them close. And if they're close to you, they're close to what you believe in, too, because the foundation you have built, the relationship you have, allows them to witness your faith in action.

In that way, even though I may not currently *Believe* (with a capital *B*), I'm probably closer to knowing God than I've ever been before. And that's because people who are close to God have also chosen to be close to me.

Jim's Epilogue

One of the things I enjoy most about working with Casper is listening to how he uses the Bible to explain his unbelief. I highly recommend you ask your non-Christian friends to do this for you.

Experience has taught me that, apart from professional Christians, most *believers* aren't exactly sure how to reconcile Matthew 7:21-23 and Matthew 10:32-33 either. Casper simply *noticed* this interpretive loophole and asked if he might be able to use it to get into heaven even though he doesn't believe in God.

On the one hand, *he says:*

> *I must* be saved, because, after all, "not everyone who says to me, 'Lord, Lord,' will enter the kingdom of heaven." I have done (or at least I work really, really hard at doing) "the will" mentioned above. I do unto others as I would have them do unto me. . . . Really, the only thing I haven't done, that separates me from the Christians in my life, is stand up and say, "Yes, I believe."

On the other hand, he says:

> But, wait . . . then I must *not* be saved, because, after all:
> "Whoever acknowledges me before others, I will also
> acknowledge before my Father in heaven."

Casper's questions tell us that non-Christians compare these
two well-known passages and, absent a preacher to "explain the
meaning of the original Greek," wonder how Christians don't
seem to be bothered by what, to them, are glaring contradictions.
From my perspective, as someone who has dedicated his life to
helping outsiders connect with Jesus, their subjective perception
of me is far more important than my subjective interpretation
of the Bible.

My Jesus did not come to earth to prove He was right. He
came to prove He was love. He didn't come just to save the world;
He came to serve the world. Saving us was "baked in" to serving us, so of course He did that as well. My Jesus was not afraid
of engaging *anyone*, be they lepers, prostitutes, tax collectors,
or Pharisees. My Jesus managed to connect with an incredibly
diverse group of humans without losing His own humanity.

If you've read the Gospels, you know that many religious
people in Jesus' time were *certain* they were on God's side, but
20/20 hindsight shows they interpreted the Bible incorrectly.
They even used the Bible to justify killing God's only Son. Their
irritation seemed to be triggered by Jesus' unfortunate habit of
being less interested in the letter of the law and more interested
in the spirit of the law. He read people's hearts. He saw their
motives.

When the Roman centurion asked Jesus to heal his servant,
Jesus said that He would come and heal him. The centurion said,
"I do not deserve to have you come under my roof. But just say
the word, and my servant will be healed" (Matthew 8:8). Jesus

was truly amazed at the generous and authentic faith of this one whom many religious people looked upon with disdain. Jesus turned to the religious crowd and insulted them by saying, "I have not found anyone in Israel with such great faith" (Matthew 8:10). Maybe it was hyperbole or maybe Jesus really meant it literally. I choose to believe the latter. Jesus saw the faith of the outsider at play and responded for what it was.

That's how I think about much of what Casper says to me. I hear the voice of Jesus in Casper's stories, challenging me to follow Jesus with greater tenacity and passion. Even when I feel offended, I try to listen because I know sometimes my Master offends my mind to get through to my heart.

THE STORY OF CHURCHRATER.COM

JIM: We have said repeatedly throughout this book that Casper and I value connecting with others above most everything else. And one way we connect with others is through ChurchRater. com. We started the website after *Jim & Casper Go to Church* came out, and hoped it would be a place where we could continue the dialog we began on our church visits. We soon found that many, *many* people wanted to share their church experiences with us and with the rest of the world. The website soon attracted a fair amount of attention from the media, and attracts new people every day. Pretty cool stuff.

In our original manuscript, we had a chapter that explained all about ChurchRater.com. We went back and forth over whether to include this somewhat off-topic discussion in the book, and in the end we decided to post it online. You can access it for free by scanning this QR code with your smartphone, or visiting the link below the code.

ChurchRater.com is a virtual case study on connecting online, so we thought online would be the best place for it. On the website, Casper and I have connected with more church visitors

www.tyndal.es/
churchrater

and church leaders than we ever could in person. We've helped church leaders better connect with visitors (both first-timers and long-time attendees). We've even helped a few leaders make some changes to their churches to help save them. (You can see why it both fits and doesn't fit this book: Saving churches is not about saving Casper, per se).

We invite you to take a look at this online appendix. As you read through it, view it for what we believe it is: a real-world example of keeping people close in spite of—or, rather, *because* of—their differences from you.

Acknowledgments

Jim: First and foremost, I want to thank Cara Highsmith for saving *Saving Casper*. Thanks to our literary agent, Esther Fedorkevich, Cara showed up just in the nick of time and got this book across the finish line. I want to thank the people who pre-read our book and offered insights that helped make it a better book. I want to thank all the people who "stayed in the room with us" as Jim and Casper forced them to travel to new places in their spiritual thought life. Finally, I want to thank Matt Casper for his willingness to keep hanging out with this Jesus freak named Jim and for calling me his friend. I'm truly honored.

Matt: Jim Henderson, thank you for inviting me on your journey and for being endlessly interested in mine. Cara Highsmith, thank you for saving *Saving Casper*. (You know that's my line, Jim!) Thanks to the fine folks at Tyndale Momentum for supporting this unusual partnership.

Discussion Guide

This guide is designed for a four-week individual or group study of *Saving Casper*. Within each week, the questions are divided by chapter so you can adjust for a shorter or longer study, if needed. Feel free to focus on the questions or issues that resonate the most with you, rather than feeling you have to cover everything; the guide is intended to be a starting point for deeper conversation and exploration.

WEEK 1: Read the preface, introduction, and chapter 1
Preface and Introduction
1. Why does Jim say we need people like Casper speaking to the church? What is your own reason for wanting to read what Casper says? How do these reasons relate to Samir Salmanovic's suggestion that atheists are "God's whistle-blowers"?
2. What is your definition of successful evangelism? What is it based on, and why? Conversely, do you think there is such a thing as *failure* in evangelism?
3. Do you agree with Jim's definitions of the "starting line" and the "finish line"? He illustrates with the story of Jesus and the Samaritan woman; what other examples in Jesus' interactions with people might support or challenge Jim's theory?

4. What has been your experience with the difficult questions that Jim says everyone who cares about evangelism will face? What is your own response to these questions?

5. Do you suffer from Evangelism Frustration Disorder? If so, in what ways? If not, what is different about your own experience?

6. Barna research shows that most unchurched people are not being pursued by anyone. Does this surprise you? Why or why not?

Chapter 1: What's Wrong with Jim?

1. Do you find yourself sharing any of the preconceived notions many Christians have about atheists? Does reading Casper's responses to these ideas change your opinion at all?

2. What is your response to Jim's scenarios 1 and 2? What are some ways you can personally leave doors open for nonbelievers to walk through in your life?

3. What do you think of how Casper answers the question: "Do atheists expect all Christians to act just like Jesus?" Does it provoke you, inspire you, unsettle you, etc.? What do you think "acting like Jesus" looks like?

4. Jim says, "I used to think that if I lost a friend in the process of evangelizing, it was okay with Jesus." Why does he no longer believe this is the outcome Jesus had in mind? What is your own opinion?

WEEK 2: Read chapters 2–4

Chapter 2: You Seem Really Nice . . . Too Bad You're Going to Hell

1. In your opinion and experience, is it okay to introduce the topic of hell into a conversation with a nonbeliever? What factors do you take into account?

2. Jim says that if Christians really mean what we say about hell, we would be living a different kind of life. Do you agree? What do you think might change?

3. Describe some ways of evangelizing "with your ears." What are its potential benefits and/or downsides?

4. Do you ever find yourself feeling defensive when talking about your faith versus others' beliefs? How do you handle it?

5. How do you reconcile the Christian mandates to both speak truth and act in love when it comes to your relationships with people who don't share your faith?

Chapter 3: Called to Question

1. Why do you think Casper's mom said she "battled" atheism? Can you relate to the struggle she describes?

2. Why do you think some people find questions uncomfortable? Do you ever avoid asking others questions about what they believe—or facing tough questions about your own faith—and if so, why? Are there any instances in Scripture when we are invited to ask questions of God?

3. What are some examples of helpful and unhelpful questions Casper and Jim give in this chapter? What would you say are the key characteristics of a helpful question?

4. Casper says that the most impactful moments for him are when someone shows care without needing recognition. Can you think of someone in your own life who models this attitude?

Chapter 4: It's All Over *Including* the Shoutin'

1. How does Casper define *tolerance*? How does it compare to your own idea of tolerance?

2. Casper admits that "the Casper of about ten years ago . . . would likely be arguing right now." Would you say your own approach toward dialogue has changed in the last ten years?

If so, how? To what extent has your faith informed those changes?

3. What might be different in your day-to-day life if you approached every interaction you have as the foundation of a relationship?

4. How would you respond to Jim's observation that "a shouting match, even among people of intelligence, yields nothing in the exchange of ideas"? Have you found this to be true?

WEEK 3: Read chapters 5–7
Chapter 5: When Bad Things Happen to Damned People

1. How do you see Casper's atheism informing his views of life and death in this chapter? What similarities and differences do they bear to your own views?

2. Todd Hunter says, "Heaven is not the goal; it's the destination." What would you say is the goal?

3. What does Casper say was helpful about his mom's church community coming alongside his family? What does he struggle with? How might Casper's insights inform the way you support others during hard times—and would there be any difference in how you navigate the situation if the others are Christians or atheists?

4. Have you ever had people like the Flanagans in your life? Is there anyone you know of who might need a "Flanagan" right now? How might you be there for that person?

5. If we all "navigate through life with an agenda," what's yours? How can you present it well? Is it really possible to have an agenda-free conversation?

Chapter 6: If One Religion Doesn't Work . . . Create Another

1. Why does Jim say, "When people like each other, the rules change"? How does his friendship with Casper reflect that?

Do you have any relationships in your own life that demonstrate this?

2. Jim says, "When it comes to religion, what you believe (in your head) far outweighs how you behave or what you put into practice." Do you agree with him that this is a characteristic of religions, including Christianity? Do you think this is the way Jesus meant for it to be? Why or why not?

3. What is Jim's idea of "Otherlyness"? Is it something you'd want to practice in your own life? If so, how can you go about doing this?

4. What is Jim's answer to the group of atheists when he is asked why he follows Jesus? What would your own answer be to that question?

5. How do Casper and Jim define freedom? How do they pursue this differently? Do you agree that "the freest people aren't chained down by what they want"?

6. Casper says, "When people try to reason with me that I should become a Christian because Jesus will set me free, . . . they lose me." Why does he say this? What might you say to Casper instead if you were having this conversation with him?

Chapter 7: Casper Saves a Christian

1. Why do you think people can get caught up in the numbers when evaluating evangelistic efforts? What are some better ways to measure success?

2. If you had been in the audience when Jim directly asked who thought Casper was going to hell, would you have raised your hand? Why or why not? Would your response be any different if Casper was not there in the room? In a situation like this, how might you reconcile being kind while also being honest about your beliefs?

3. Casper says that the promise of heaven and the threat of

hell don't bring him closer to becoming a Christian, because he doesn't believe either exists. What is your reaction to his statement? Why do you think Christians often share their faith by starting with a discussion of the afterlife?

4. What was Casper's response to the woman who called him evil? What was his response to the woman who asked him how to save the church? What can we learn from these interactions?

5. Moving on the "judgment meter" is easier said than done. How do we start from a place of relationship instead of judgment when communicating with those who don't share our beliefs?

WEEK 4: Read chapters 8–9 and Casper's Conclusion and Jim's Epilogue
Chapter 8: Why I Am *Currently* a Christian

1. Why does Casper say he's currently an atheist? By the same logic, would you consider yourself currently a Christian? Why or why not?

2. Has your own spiritual experience been more of a journey or a jump? Why do you think we emphasize the "Eureka" moment if transformation is a process?

3. Casper believes that the more people you connect with who hold different views from your own, the more you will grow personally. Do you agree? With whom have you connected recently who has stretched and challenged you by their different beliefs? Are there any such people in your life with whom you would like to connect more? How can you go about doing that?

4. What is the difference between having strong beliefs and elevating those beliefs to the point of worshiping certainty? How can we recognize the latter?

Chapter 9: How to Save an Atheist

1. Which question and answer in this chapter resonates most with you? Why? Are there any other questions you wish Casper had answered?
2. What does Casper say is the best way to keep him "open" to faith, and why? Does his comment inspire you to engage differently with nonbelievers?
3. What do you think of the marketing aspect of evangelism? Do you agree with Casper's pull-rather-than-push strategy? How can you find ways to get "your prospects to ask the questions"?
4. Why do you think atheists are "supposedly the least trusted group in America"? What is the difference between an atheist and what Casper calls an anti-theist?
5. Why does Casper prefer the terms *constructive* and *destructive* versus *right* and *wrong*? Do you agree or disagree with his reasoning? Can you think of situations in which each might be used appropriately?

Casper's Conclusion

1. Instead of starting with "the end" or heaven/hell, what does Casper suggest as a better way to start a dialogue with an atheist—and why?
2. What do you think it takes to be "saved"? Do you agree with Casper that it's confusing or is there something he's missing? Can someone be "saved secretly"? If you were talking with Casper, is there anything you'd want to contribute to his analysis of what it means to be saved?
3. Casper asks, "Is there biblical support for giving up on me?" Why does he ask this question? How would you answer it?

Jim's Epilogue

1. Jim says that sometimes God offends his mind to get

through to his heart. Has this ever happened to you? How can you learn through times where you feel offended?

2. What is Jim's attitude toward nonbelievers? What is Casper's attitude toward Christians? Overall, what have their mutual attitudes throughout the book taught you about connecting with people of different beliefs?

About Jim Henderson

Jim Henderson is fascinated with the power of listening. He invites people to eavesdrop on his interviews with Outsiders of all stripes to hear what they think about spiritual matters. These conversations motivated Jim to write a number of books, including *Jim & Casper Go to Church* (with Matt Casper), a book that documents the journey of a Christian and an atheist visiting a variety of churches together. His production company, Jim Henderson Presents, creates live events designed to "take Jesus public."

Jim holds a DMin in transformational leadership and has been featured in the *Wall Street Journal* and *USA Today*, and on Fox Television and *This American Life* with Ira Glass.

About Matt Casper

Matt Casper has had more than fifty jobs. One of which is writing books. *Jim & Casper Go to Church* was his first full-length book. *Saving Casper* is his second. He has also had various essays, reviews, and ephemera published, online and off, and has been a copywriter for fifteen years.

But back to the fifty jobs: Matt has also been a landscaper, e-mail marketer, dishwasher, greenskeeper, waiter, retail clerk, researcher, messenger (foot and van), musician, ice cream server, bug killer, copyeditor (different than a copywriter), assembly line worker, laborer, legal temp, and about thirty other things. All of which he plans to write about someday. He is also an atheist who attended a Catholic college and who has visited dozens of US churches. And he has played his own tunes in bands for more than twenty years ("garagey, melodic, scrappy pop music," he says).

Above everything else, Matt is a dad, and he recommends fatherhood to anyone reliable, devoted, creative, and driven, who is also willing and able to be the most responsible "kid" their own kids would know and—most important—capable of selfless love.

And three more things Matt really enjoys: 1) enumerated lists, 2) starting sentences with conjunctions, and 3) writing about himself in the third person.

Notes

1. Hemant later wrote a book about the experience titled *I Sold My Soul on eBay* (Waterbrook, 2007).
2. Samir Salmanovic, *It's Really All About God* (San Francisco: Jossey-Bass, 2009), 188.
3. Ibid., 188–189.
4. George Barna, *Re-churching the Unchurched* (Ventura, CA: Issachar Resources, 2000).
5. Dan Harris, "Young Americans Losing Their Religion," ABC news, May 6, 2009, http://abcnews.go.com/Politics/story?id=7513343&page=1.
6. James Davison Hunter, *To Change the World* (New York: Oxford University Press, 2010), 26.
7. Nick Spencer and Peter Neilson, *Journeys and Stories: Finding Faith in Scotland Today* (London Institute for Contemporary Christianity, 2006), 59.
8. Michael Frost and Alan Hirsch, *The Shaping of Things to Come: Innovation and Mission for the 21st Century* (Peabody, MA: Hendrickson, 2003), 99.
9. John Finney, *Finding Faith Today* (London: Bible Society, 1992), 25.
10. http://www.brainyquote.com/quotes/quotes/a/alberteins162052.html
11. Charles Seife, *Zero: The Biography of a Dangerous Idea* (New York: Penguin, 2000), 19.
12. Ibid., 25.
13. Ibid., 5.
14. Joan Chittister, *Called to Question: A Spiritual Memoir* (Oxford: Rowman & Littlefield, 2004), 14.
15. Ibid., 54.
16. David Bosch, *Transforming Mission: Paradigm Shifts in Theology of Mission* (Maryknoll, NY: Orbis, 2011), 495.
17. http://www.brainyquote.com/quotes/keywords/shouting.html
18. Stephen Prothero, *God is Not One: The Eight Rival Religions that Run the World—and Why Their Differences Matter* (New York: HarperOne, 2010), 109.
19. http://requisite_danger.bluecastle.us/2009/04/22/conversation-with-todd-hunter-part-two/
20. John Lennon, "Imagine," 1971.
21. Shout-out to my good friend and mentor Brian McLaren for teaching me this.
22. *The Big Kahuna*, 1999. Screenplay by Roger Rueff; directed by John Swanbeck.

23. http://washingtonfamilyranch.younglife.org/Pages/Travel-Information.aspx

24. Kathryn Schulz, *Being Wrong: Adventures in the Margin of Error* (New York: HarperCollins, 2010), 107–110.

25. Recovering alcoholics say I am (currently) an alcoholic and staying sober one day at a time. This used to irritate me because it seemed so uncertain. Now I identify with them. I follow Jesus one day at a time. (To be completely honest, it's more like sixty seconds at a time.)

26. "Only 14 percent report their conversion as an *experience* or *event* that occurred at one point in time. The vast majority of respondents report coming to faith as a process that took several weeks to a year (32 percent), a period of several years (24 percent), or even many years (30 percent). It is interesting to reflect how well these data fit with the findings on the importance of relationships over some of the more traditional evangelistic program techniques." (*Vision New England Recent Convert Study*, January 2007), 11.

27. "In the twenty-first century alone, religion has toppled the Bamiyan statues of the Buddha in Afghanistan and the Twin Towers in New York City. . . . But religion also gave us abolitionism and the civil rights movement." Stephen Prothero, *God is Not One: The Eight Rival Religions that Run the World* (New York: HarperOne, 2010), 89.

28. Kathryn Schulz, *Being Wrong: Adventures in the Margin of Error* (New York: HarperCollins, 2010), 104.

29. George G. Hunter, *The Celtic Way of Evangelism: How Christianity Can Reach the West . . . Again* (Nashville: Abingdon, 2010), 108.

30. http://www.ericdemay.com/quotes/quote-17

31. http://quoteinvestigator.com/2012/01/24/future-has-arrived. Gibson is also known for originating the term *cyberspace*.

32. Felix Hoover, "Ohio Church Reviewer Dies at 82," *Columbus Dispatch*, March 28, 2006.

33. Roger Van Oech is the author of the best-selling creativity classics *A Whack on the Side of the Head*; *A Kick in the Seat of the Pants*; and *Expect the Unexpected*; and the popular Creative Whack Pack and Innovative Whack Pack card decks.

Online Discussion *guide*

TAKE *your* TYNDALE READING EXPERIENCE *to the* NEXT LEVEL

A FREE discussion guide for this book is available at bookclubhub.net, perfect for sparking conversations in your book group or for digging deeper into the text on your own.

www.bookclubhub.net

You'll also find free discussion guides for other Tyndale books, e-newsletters, e-mail devotionals, virtual book tours, and more!

"Is this what Jesus told you guys to do?"

Light shows, fog machines, worship bands, offering plates—is this what Jesus intended? Atheist Matt Casper wants to know.

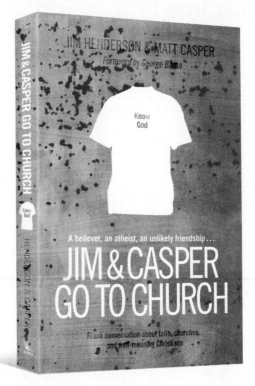

Longtime Christian Jim Henderson realized that he had no idea how a nonbeliever might interpret a usual Sunday service . . . or what might inspire him or her to come back.

So he decided to ask! Jim invited an atheist—Matt Casper—to visit twelve leading churches with him and give the "first impression" perspective of a nonbeliever. Follow along with Jim and Casper on their visits, and eavesdrop as they discuss what they found. Their articulate, sometimes humorous, and always insightful dialogue offers Christians a view of an environment where we've become overly comfortable: the church.

ISBN 978-1-4143-5858-1

CP0522

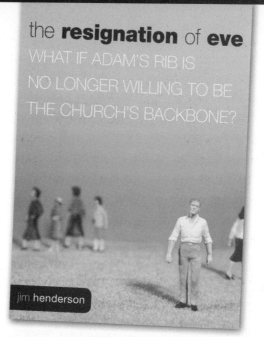

the **resignation** of **eve**

WHAT IF ADAM'S RIB IS NO LONGER WILLING TO BE THE CHURCH'S BACKBONE?

jim henderson

In talking with women around the country, Jim Henderson has come to believe there is an epidemic of quiet, even sad resignation among dedicated Christian women who are feeling overworked and under-valued in the church. As a result, many women are discouraged. Some, particularly young women, respond by leaving the organized church . . . or walking away from the faith altogether.

What does this mean for your church and for the body of Christ as a whole?

Containing personal interviews with women and new research from George Barna, *The Resignation of Eve* is a must-read, conversation-starting book for women who have been engaged in the church, as well as for their pastors and ministry leaders.

ISBN 978-1-4143-3730-2

CP0524